PROCLAMATION COMMENTARIES

Second Edition
Revised and Enlarged   Gerhard Krodel, *Editor*

Jack Dean Kingsbury

FORTRESS PRESS   PHILADELPHIA

Second printing 1987

Library of Congress Cataloging-in-Publication Data

Kingsbury, Jack Dean.
Matthew.

(Proclamation commentaries)
Bibliography: p.
Includes index.
1. Bible. N.T. Matthew—Criticism, interpretation, etc. 2. Bible. N.T. Matthew—Homiletical use.
I. Title. II. Series.
BS2575.2.K47 1986   226′.2006   86–45212
ISBN 0–8006–0597–7

3246H87 Printed in the United States of America 1–597

To
Frederick & Lois Danker
Paul & Ruth Manz
Norman & Jeannette Kretzmann

CONTENTS

PREFACE

To revise a book is to have the opportunity to scrutinize it afresh and to bring it abreast of recent advances in research. Such has been the case with this revision of *Matthew*. In addition, the opportunity for revision has also made it possible to introduce innumerable minor changes into the text aimed at clarifying some statement or argument or simply making the book more readable.

Since the rise of the method known as redaction criticism following World War II, more progress has perhaps been made toward gaining a better understanding of the respective Gospels than in any other comparable period of time. The present book is a study in that form of redaction criticism often called composition criticism. The intention is to ascertain what is characteristically Matthean not by attempting to distinguish between tradition and redaction but by examining the First Gospel as a unified whole.

The manner in which the study progresses is clearly indicated by the chapter headings. Thus, chapter 1 presents a brief overview of the history of Matthean research in this century and explains how redaction, or composition, criticism is both similar to and different from other interpretive methods. It also sketches the particularities of the approach to Matthew taken here. Chapter 2 deals with Matthew's portrait of Jesus by discussing both his person and his mission. Next, because what is unique about Jesus in Matthean perspective is that in him God draws near to humankind with his end-time rule, chapter 3 explores Matthew's understanding of God's rule, or kingdom. And finally, because the Matthean Jesus is also one who calls disciples and founds the church, chapter 4 concerns itself with Matthew's understanding of the community of the disciples.

Mention should doubtless be made of specific ways in which this revised and enlarged version differs from its predecessor. Chapter 1 has been heavily reworked. Two new sections have been added, namely, "Biography as a Genre of Ancient Literature," and "A Comparison [of Redaction Criticism] with Literary Criticism." The section entitled "A Redaction-Critical Approach in Outline" has also been edited in the interest of streamlining the argument.

Chapter 2 has likewise undergone considerable change. The sections on "The Mission of the Son of God" and on "Jesus as the Son of Man" have either been largely or completely recast. Changes of a substantive nature have also been made in three other sections: "Jesus Messiah, the Son of God"; "Jesus as the Son of David"; and "Jesus as Lord."

In chapters 3 and 4, the changes introduced have been less dramatic. Still, as in all the chapters, the number of footnotes has been greatly increased, to remove biblical references from the body of the book (and thus enhance its readability) and to allow for additional references to more recent scholarly literature. As regards the latter, it ought also be observed that the annotated bibliography at the end of the book has likewise been significantly enlarged. Even at this, however, it remains a "selected bibliography."

My heartfelt thanks upon publication of this revised version go to more people than I could ever single out by name. Nonetheless, I should like to remember in print such as the following: the many pastors and students who, upon reading the original version, responded to it with insightful praise or blame; to Gerhard Krodel, editor of the Proclamation Commentaries Series, for inviting me to reassess the original book and improve upon it; to John A. Hollar, at Fortress Press, for guiding yet another manuscript through to publication; to Keith H. Reeves, my graduate assistant, for preparing the index; and especially of course to my wife Barbara, whose grace, beauty, and humor never fail to buoy the spirit and quicken the mind.

Jack Dean Kingsbury

CHAPTER ONE

TOWARD AN UNDERSTANDING
OF MATTHEW

The goal of this book is to set forth Matthew's understanding of Jesus, of the kingdom of heaven, and of discipleship. To deal adequately with these themes, however, one must have a firm notion of the nature and purpose of the Gospel. Is it, for example, of the nature of a biography that was written to detail for Christians the life and ministry of Jesus of Nazareth? Or is it of the nature of a manual that was meant to instruct Christian converts or indeed church leaders in matters deemed to be fundamental to Christian faith? Or, just the opposite, is it of the nature of inspirational literature intended to stir Christians to action by picturing graphically the rewards of faithfulness and the penalties of unfaithfulness? Or, while containing elements of all the above, is it perhaps best understood as something else written for still a different purpose?

Theoretically, there are two ways to learn of the nature and purpose of Matthew's Gospel. The one is to attempt to cull such information from the writings of the early Church Fathers. This attempt has often been made, but without clear results. The second way is to study the Gospel itself. This is the course that will be followed in this book.

Matthew's Gospel has been studied more carefully in the past hundred years than ever before. Especially since World War II, scholars have devoted an immense amount of attention to it, and great strides have been made toward gaining a better understanding of it. The object of this chapter, therefore, is to probe the question of the nature and purpose of Matthew's Gospel with the aid of modern scholarship.

The Biographical Approach

Biography as Historical Reportage

Last century and in the early part of this century, the prevailing view of history was "positivistic" in nature. On this view the historian, through a

1

critical reading of the ancient documents, endeavors to reconstruct the "facts" and describe "how things really were."

In the area of NT studies, one of the major preoccupations of scholars was the quest of the historical Jesus. The goal was to sift through the contents of the Gospels in order to establish an outline of Jesus' ministry according to time and place, and to determine both how he thought of himself and of his mission and what his teaching was concerning the kingdom of God. Because it was generally conceded that Mark's Gospel was the first to have been written, and because it furthermore seemed to contain primitive traditions, scholars quite naturally gravitated toward it as the most reliable source for factual data concerning Jesus. Conversely, they were much less inclined to involve Matthew and Luke in the quest, since the latter two in their judgment are more literary in character and appear to build on Mark. Basically, they looked to them for sayings of Jesus Mark does not have. The result was that for a time Mark received by far the lion's share of scholarly attention, and Matthew and Luke receded into the background.

Still, during these years there were some scholars of note who stoutly defended Matthean priority. They insisted that the First Gospel could be traced, if not directly then through the translation into Greek of an Aramaic original, to the hand of the apostle Matthew (cf. 9:9; 10:3). Hence, it is the First Gospel, they maintained, that is in substance the earliest. In it one has access to eyewitness reports from the time of Jesus.

Not surprisingly, it was from among this circle of scholars advocating the priority of Matthew that the more imposing Matthean commentaries came.[1] Moreover, it was within this circle of scholars that Matthew was also regarded as having the character of biography. Unfortunately, the concept of biography that was in vogue at this time did not derive so much from the study of ancient biographical writings as from the modern notion that biography is to be equated with historical reportage. The method of interpretation that is based on this notion is known as the historical-biographical approach. The distinguishing feature of this approach is the belief that Matthew is of the nature of a chronicle, or documentary, the purpose of which is to present a relatively continuous and detailed account of events as they actually took place in the life and ministry of the earthly Jesus.

As applied to Matthew, therefore, the historical-biographical approach constituted in effect an attempt to utilize the data of the Gospel to achieve the objectives of the quest of the historical Jesus. Indeed, appeal for this approach could even be made to the Gospel itself. The opening words, it was claimed, are to be translated "The Book of the History of Jesus Christ . . ." (1:1; cf., e.g., Gen. 37:2 [RSV]). These words, purported to be the title of the Gospel, were said to prove that it was Matthew's intention to write a "history book about Jesus the Messiah."[2]

Convinced that the First Gospel should be read as an objective report on the life of Jesus, the proponents of the historical-biographical approach attempted to draft a factually sound portrait of Jesus. In general, Jesus stands out in this portrait as the Prophet who proclaimed the gospel of the kingdom and as the Teacher who made known the will of God (4:23; 9:35; chaps. 5—7). Calling disciples to follow him (4:18-22; 9:9; 10:2-4), he wandered about Galilee instructing and healing the people (4:23-25; 9:35; 11:5). In order to gather from Israel a new community, he dispatched his disciples on a missionary journey (9:35—10:42). Owing to the fickleness of the crowds and the enmity of the Jewish leaders, Jesus recognized that only death lay before him (chaps. 11—12). Hence, he withdrew from public (12:15) and embarked on private journeys with his disciples, preparing them for what lay ahead (chaps. 14—20). Finally, knowing that his time had come (cf. 16:21), he journeyed to Jerusalem, whereupon the events surrounding his death and resurrection took place (chaps. 26—28).

While there is perhaps nothing implausible about this outline of the life of Jesus per se, a prominent feature of the writings of those who took a historical-biographical approach to Matthew's Gospel is the great amount of space they devote to the filling in of the chronological and psychological gaps they encountered in the text. To illustrate this, consider merely two facets of the story of the temptation (4:1-11).[3] Thus, how is one to understand that Jesus did not become hungry until *after* he had fasted forty days and forty nights (4:2)? This was the case, we are told, because during this time Jesus was caught up in such a state of spiritual exhilaration that he was not susceptible to pangs of hunger. Or how exactly is one to conceive of the devil as *taking* Jesus to the holy city and *setting* him on the pinnacle of the temple (4:5)? Since the devil is a spirit, what happened, we learn, is that he momentarily took such control of Jesus' senses that Jesus experienced dizziness and only imagined himself to be standing atop the temple. The point is, neither of these explanations has any basis in the text; both arise from an effort to construe the text as objective historical description.

The latter statement is tantamount already to an evaluation of the historical-biographical approach to Matthew's Gospel. What is one to make of it?

The overwhelming evidence is that none of the Gospels is of the nature of biography understood as historical reportage. The Gospels were not meant to be "literary archives." They do contain traditions that go back to the life and times of Jesus. But they are not to be looked upon as if each were a string of "verbal photographs" taken by family or disciples during the course of Jesus' life.

A look at the text of Matthew substantiates this judgment. The first thing to observe is that it is precisely many of those details which are, to our modern way of thinking, essential to good biography which are in especially short supply. For example, we are not told in which year Jesus was born or in which year he died. Neither is any mention made of the location of his tomb. And nothing is said about the length of his ministry, which is also true of that of John the Baptist.

Other personal details are likewise conspicuously absent. Following the infancy narratives (chaps. 1—2), the years that separate the early childhood of Jesus from his baptism as an adult (3:13-17) are passed over in silence. We are left in the dark about the school years of Jesus, about his intellectual development, and about the formation of his character. No description is given of his person, and his habits, mannerisms, and "likes and dislikes" are not discussed.

Neither do we catch a glimpse of Jesus' life at home. The friends of his youth and his relatives find no place in the gospel-story, and even references to Joseph and Mary and to his brothers and sisters can better be accounted for on literary and theological, rather than on purely historical, grounds (cf. chaps. 1—2; 12:46-50; 13:53-58). As an adult, Jesus is reported as moving from "Nazareth" to "Capernaum" (4:13), which is described as "his own city" (9:1), and it may be that he is thought of as having a "house" there.[4] But the text does not elaborate on these terse remarks.

Except for Peter and Judas at best, even the disciples, the closest associates of Jesus, do not stand out as profiled individuals. A list of their names is given (10:2-4), and now and again special mention is made of "Matthew" (9:9), of "Andrew" (4:18), and of "James" and "John."[5] But beyond such information as that Matthew may have been a "toll collector" (9:9),[6] that Andrew, James, and John were "fishermen" (4:18-22), and that James and John seem also to have shared the ambitions of their mother (20:20–28), there is little of a historical nature to be learned of the individual disciples.

If the First Gospel has little to say of the disciples as individuals, it has next to nothing to say of the other characters that dot its pages. Most of these persons do not so much as bear a name, passing before the reader merely as "the Magi" (2:1, 7), "a leper" (8:2), "a centurion" (8:5), Peter's "mother-in-law" (8:14), "a scribe" (8:19), "two demoniacs" (8:28), "a paralytic" (9:2), "disciples of John" (9:14; 11:2), "a ruler" (9:18), "a woman" (9:20), "two blind men" (9:27; 20:30), "a dumb demoniac" (9:32; cf. 12:22), "a Canaanite woman" (15:22), "a man" (17:14), "the boy" (17:18), "a child" (18:2), "the young man" (19:22), "the mother of the sons of Zebedee" (20:20; 27:56), "a lawyer" (22:35), and so on. Other characters are indeed introduced by name, but to all intents and purposes they, too, remain people without profile: "Archelaus" (2:22), "Caiaphas" (26:3, 57), "Simon the leper" (26:6), "Simon of Cyrene" (27:32), "Mary Magdalene" (27:56, 61; 28:1), "Mary the mother of James and Joseph" (27:56, 61; 28:1), and "Joseph of Arimathea" (27:57).

Nor is it any different with the enemies of Jesus. "Herod" and "Pilate" stand out to some degree as personalities. But even the name "Herod" is deceptive, since the text leaves it up to the reader to distinguish between Herod the Great (chap. 2) and Herod Antipas (14:1–12). The leaders of the Jews, in turn, appear as stereotyped groups. They confront the reader most often as the "Pharisees," the "scribes," the "scribes and Pharisees," the "Pharisees and Sadducees," the "chief priests," or the "chief priests and the elders (of the people)." Outside the passion narrative, they arrive on the scene suddenly and most often without motivation, and vanish again just as quickly. And while the people among whom Jesus carries out his ministry are depicted as assuming a neutral or even positive attitude toward him until his arrest (26:47, 55), they simply remain the anonymous masses throughout the Gospel, the "crowd(s)."

Consequently, a survey of the biographical detail of Matthew's Gospel by no means leaves the impression that it is the result of historical or spectatorial recollection of the earthly life of Jesus. How do things stand as far as the chronological and topographical detail is concerned?

Chronologically, Matthew marks the passing of time with a series of literary expressions that invite comment only because they are so vague and indefinite. Thus, in any number of passages it is the mere particle "and" that removes in time one event from another (cf. 4:23; 9:35: *"And* he went about all Galilee . . ."). In ninety instances it is the adverb "then," and frequently it is the circumstantial participle (cf. 5:1; 9:36: "And *when* he saw the crowds . . ."; 12:46: "And *while* he was yet speaking to the crowds . . ."). In still other passages the indistinct prepositional phrase performs the same function: "from that time on";[7] "at that time";[8] "at that hour";[9] "from that hour";[10] "on that day";[11] and "from that day" (22:46).

Topographically, the various settings in which Matthew depicts Jesus as discharging his ministry are likewise bland and for the most part imprecise. One encounters Jesus, for example, at the "Jordan" river (3:13), in the "desert" (4:1), on "a [the] mountain,"[12] "beside the Sea of Galilee" (4:18; 13:1), in "their synagogue(s),"[13] at "home,"[14] in a "boat" (13:2), "on the way" (20:17), going on or withdrawing "from there,"[15] and "in the region(s)" of the Gadarenes, of Tyre and Sidon, of Caesarea Philippi, or of Judea across the Jordan (8:28; 15:21; 16:13; 19:1). Apart from the passion narrative and references to the dwelling in Capernaum, the most exact Matthew becomes in identifying any given setting is when he informs the reader that Jesus is in the "house of Peter" (8:14), in or near a particular city ("Bethlehem," "Capernaum," "Bethphage," "Nazareth," "Jericho," "Jerusalem"), in the "temple" (21:12, 23), or on "the Mount of Olives" (24:3).

The paucity of biographical detail in the First Gospel and the imprecise manner in which Matthew works with chronological and topographical data are in themselves strong indications that Matthew has not approached his materials from a historical-biographical point of view as conceived by the modern mind. But hand in hand with this there is also the blatant disregard of other matters that would, to modern thinking, be of importance to any historical-biographical approach to the life of Jesus. The following examples illustrate this.

In connection with the missionary discourse that Jesus delivers to his disciples in preparation for their journey to the "lost sheep of the house of Israel" (10:5b–42), Matthew writes that Jesus "sent out" the twelve (10:5a). Still, once Jesus has finished the discourse, Matthew says nothing whatever about the disciples' actually undertaking this journey about which Jesus has spoken to them at such length. Mention is made neither of their departure nor of their return. In Mark, by contrast, both departure and return are duly noted (6:7–13, 30). If Matthew saw it as his task to write a life of Jesus in the modern sense of the term, his procedure at this juncture is baffling. But suppose that this was not his purpose. Suppose that this discourse of Jesus and its setting were of significance to him because they are of literary and theological relevance: they treat of the "Christian" mission directed first toward Israel (10:5b–6) and subsequently also toward the nations (cf. 10:18) and of the trials the followers of Jesus can always expect to endure and of the cost and reward of discipleship. But if Matthew's procedure in 9:35—10:42 has been dictated by literary and theological and not simply historical considerations, then it is perfectly comprehensible. He had no need to dwell on the departure and the return of the twelve, because with the completion of Jesus' discourse he had made his point.

A second example has to do with Matthew's portrait of the leaders of Israel. Five times he makes reference to the "Pharisees and Sadducees" as to a single group (3:7; 16:1, 6, 11, 12). What is so striking about this is the fact that, in the days of Jesus, the Pharisees and the Sadducees constituted two distinct "parties" with sharply contrasting views and theologies. The Pharisees were progressive, a party among the people. Their goal was that Israel should become the righteous nation of the covenant, and to this end they taught compliance with the so-called tradition of the elders (cf. 15:2), a code of conduct that effectively adapted the law of Moses to later times and changing demands. The Sadducees, on the other hand, were a wealthy, conservative party that was concentrated in Jerusalem and made up of aristocratic families of patrician and priestly stock. They refused adherence to the Pharisees' tradition of the elders, advocated a rigorous application of the law of Moses to the life of the nation, and in general espoused a political and religious policy including cooperation with the Romans which was aimed at preserving the status quo. The question is, what prompted Matthew to treat these two parties as one group?

This question cannot be answered satisfactorily on a purely historical basis. The reason is that Matthew's procedure in this regard is, again, literarily and theologically motivated. At 3:7 he has John the Baptist call the "Pharisees and Sadducees" a "brood of vipers," and in 12:34 and 23:33 it is Jesus who applies this same epithet, respectively, to the "Pharisees" (12:24) and to the "scribes and Pharisees" (23:27). The point is this: Matthew was not concerned to distinguish historically, in terms of the days of

Jesus, between particular factions of the leaders of Israel; within his gospel-story, they all stand forth as representatives of a monolithic front that stands implacably opposed to Jesus. Hence, the way in which Matthew has dealt with Israelite leaders of whatever stripe is governed by the firm conviction that they are the epitome of this "evil and adulterous generation" (12:38–39; 16:1, 4). Once this is understood, one can see why it is that the "Pharisees and Sadducees" should present themselves in the First Gospel as a single group.

Matthew's intent to work literarily and theologically with traditional materials, not just historically, furthermore reflects itself in his portrait of Jesus and of the disciples. Take, for instance, the manner in which persons address Jesus in the First Gospel. In Mark, Jesus is called "rabbi" or "teacher," equivalent terms of human respect, both by the disciples and those who come to him in faith,[16] and by the traitor Judas (14:45), a rich stranger (10:17, 20), a scribe (12:32), and enemies (12:14, 19). In Matthew's Gospel, by contrast, only Judas, a stranger, and the opponents of Jesus address him as "rabbi" or "teacher."[17] When his disciples or persons of faith appeal to him, they do so as "Lord," acknowledging thereby that he is one of exalted station who wields divine authority.[18] This careful differentiation between "believers" on the one hand and "outsiders" and "opponents" on the other as regards the manner in which they address Jesus cannot be squared with "things as they really were" in the life of Jesus. It admirably shows how Matthew has reshaped earlier traditions in line with the beliefs and experiences of his post-Easter church.

A glance at Matthew's portrait of the disciples corroborates the truth of this assertion. In Mark, the disciples are depicted during the ministry of Jesus as being "without understanding" and in this sense "hard of heart."[19] And in both Luke and John it is said that it was not until the resurrection that the disciples were led to grasp the deeper significance of the person and ministry of Jesus.[20]

From the witness of the NT, it is surely correct historically to say that the disciples did not perceive aright what had transpired in the life of Jesus until they had gazed upon this life from the vantage point of Easter. Each in his own fashion, Mark, Luke, and John attest to this circumstance. Matthew, however, can be seen to fly in the face of it. He pictures the disciples as persons who can understand. In principle, they have "eyes that do see" and "ears that do hear" the "mysteries of the kingdom of heaven."[21] Except for their inability to grasp why Jesus must die and what the implications of his destiny are for discipleship (cf. 16:21–28), their ignorance is temporary in nature, until Jesus has had opportunity to explain the matter.[22] How is such insight on the part of the disciples to be accounted for? The explanation is that Matthew has endowed the pre-Easter disciples of his story with understanding that, historically speaking, the flesh-and-blood disciples did not attain until after Easter. Matthew has impressed upon the tradition the perspective of his own literary and theological tenets.

The preceding are four illustrations of the way in which Matthew has worked literarily and theologically with traditional materials. When one considers that the historical-biographical approach to the First Gospel rests on the premise that Matthew wrote primarily as a historian endeavoring to compile for all time a chronicle of the life and times of Jesus, it is not difficult to recognize the fundamental inappropriateness of this approach. As will be seen, Matthew was highly respectful of the past. But he stands forth first of all as an author and theologian. What this means, finally, is that he did not compose his Gospel as one whose goal was to repristinate the days of Jesus prior to crucifixion, but as one who aimed to tell of the person, ministry, and passion of Jesus from the standpoint of post-Easter faith.

Biography as a Genre of Ancient Literature

Of itself the term "biography" denotes a specific genre, or type, of literature. In designating the Gospels as biography and then defining biography as historical reportage, scholars of the nineteenth and early twentieth centuries both narrowed the meaning of the term and gave it a distinctively modern coloration. In the last twenty years, however, there has been a steady growth in interest among scholars in the notion of biography as a type of ancient Greco-Roman literature. In particular, scholars have posed two questions: Do the canonical Gospels in fact belong to the genre of ancient Greco-Roman biography? And if it be judged that they do so belong, what has one gained in making this determination?

The necessity of asking whether the canonical Gospels can in fact be classified as ancient biography stems from the circumstance that, since the 1920s, a virtual consensus of opinion has held sway in scholarly circles which affirms that the canonical Gospels are, as far as the matter of genre is concerned, unique (sui generis).[23] The reasoning behind this opinion runs like this. Following Easter, the message Christians proclaimed, that is, the kerygma, focused on the cross and resurrection of Jesus (1 Cor. 11:23–26; 15:3–7). In addition, sayings of Jesus were gathered, individually or in groups, as well as stories about him. The one who created the type of literature known as the Gospel was the evangelist Mark. A member of the Hellenistic, as opposed to the Palestinian, wing of the church, Mark compiled, combined, and arranged traditions of the words of Jesus and stories about him so as to proclaim the earthly Jesus as the Son of God and Lord he and his fellow Christians worshiped. On balance, therefore, the Gospel, as a literary creation, is the product of the "imminent urge to development" which lay in the early Christian kerygma and in early Christian worship.[24] Strictly speaking, the Gospel cannot even be termed a "literary genre," because it is without analogy in the Greco-Roman world.[25] Indeed, the best one can do to find an analogy to the Gospel as a type of literature is to look, not to "high" forms of literature such as Hellenistic biography, but to works of popular or folk literature, that is, to materials which are collections of loosely joined words and deeds of well-known personages and which do not give evidence of advanced compositional technique.[26]

Why has this view that the canonical Gospels are, as a type of literature, unique *(sui generis)* increasingly lost credibility among some scholars as of late? The answer is multiple. For one thing, because this view conceives of the Gospel genre as being the natural outgrowth of the earliest kerygma of the cross and resurrection, it takes almost no account of what it means for the Gospel writers to have been "authors."[27] For another thing, this view likewise provides no adequate explanation as to exactly how the kerygma of Jesus' cross and resurrection came to be "elongated" so as to give rise to a genre that in form resembles a "life of Jesus."[28] And third, in advancing the claim that the Gospel genre is not the adaptation of a genre already existing in the Greco-Roman world but is without analogy, this view ignores the theoretical problem of how any literary creation that is so new and therefore alien to its contemporary culture could communicate meaningfully to people at home within this culture.[29]

Spurred by perceived weaknesses in the consensus opinion such as these, a number of scholars have explored the various genres of Greco-Roman literature with an eye to ascertaining whether there is not sufficient affinity between the canonical Gospels and any given genre as to warrant classifying the Gospels as such. Almost without exception, these scholars point to ancient biography as being that genre. The reason is that, as Graham Stanton has argued, the Gospels compare favorably in important respects to ancient biographical writings. On the one hand, the Gospels, like ancient biography, are largely devoid of the preoccupation with "chronological precision, historical background, personal appearance and character development" which tends to be the mark of modern biography.[30] On the other hand, the Gospels, in analogy to ancient biography, are intended to "portray the life and character of Jesus," not solely out of historical interest, but in order to proclaim Jesus even while sketching the sort of person he was.[31]

Convinced that the canonical Gospels lie within the generical orbit of ancient biography, some scholars have pressed further and attempted to identify the sub-type to which they best correspond. The following are four suggestions that have been advanced. First, the Gospels are of the nature of "popular biography," the purpose of which is to make known the personality and message of Jesus so as to promote Christian missionary efforts.[32] Second, the Gospels are of the nature of the "aretalogy," the purpose of which is to render account of the remarkable career of an impressive teacher and thus impart moral instruction.[33] Third, the Gospels are of the nature of "biography which aims to dispel a false image and establish a true one."[34] And fourth, the Gospels are of the nature of the "encomium," the purpose of which is to evoke the praise and emulation of Jesus.[35]

As far as the Gospel of Matthew itself is concerned, Philip Shuler has adopted William Farmer's suggestion and argued that Matthew reflects the pattern which identifies it as belonging to the genre of "encomium biography."[36] In support of this contention, Shuler makes three basic points. As in encomium, the *topics* Matthew treats at the beginning of his Gospel are meant to define Jesus' identity and indicate his greatness, even as the topics he treats in connection with Jesus' death and resurrection are meant to glorify him and to elicit from the reader praise of him and faith in him. The literary *techniques* Matthew has employed are such as (a) to organize his materials according to "themes" and, overall, in the form of a "life of Jesus," and (b) to make use of "amplification," which is a device calculated to enhance the admirable qualities of Jesus, and "comparison," which is a device calculated to stress the unparalleled excellence of Jesus over all other characters. And the dual *purpose* Matthew intends to accomplish with his Gospel is to present a compelling portrait of the crucified and risen Messiah on the one hand and to inspire in the reader emulation of this Messiah on the other.

If the scholarly world could be made to grant that the canonical Gospels, and in particular Matthew, are of the nature of ancient biography, what would one thereby gain? Perhaps the greatest gain one would achieve is simply to surmount scholarly antipathy against designating the canonical Gospels as biography. Given the fact that scholars in the nineteenth and early twentieth centuries defined biography in modern terms to mean the writing of a continuous and detailed account of events as they really happened in the life of the earthly Jesus, and given the fact that the consensus opinion among scholars since the 1920s has been that the canonical Gospels are generically unique *(sui generis)*, it is not surprising that scholars have for the most part refused to associate the canonical Gospels with the genre of biography, even ancient biography. Consequently, if such scholarly refusal were to be overcome, it would in fact constitute an achievement of no small proportions. In this study, Matthew's Gospel will be construed as a "story of the life of Jesus." In this limited sense, therefore, the Gospel will be identified with the genre of ancient biography.

A second gain one would achieve, were it granted that the canonical Gospels are of the nature of ancient biography, is also largely negative in character, namely, in specifying what the canonical Gospels are, one is at the same time specifying what they are not. Generically, the canonical Gospels are not, say, an "apocalypse" like the apocryphal Epistle of the Apostles, or a "sayings source" like Q or the Gospel of Thomas, or a pure "aretalogy" like the reputed signs source of John's Gospel, or a "manual of discipline" like that found at Qumran, or "historical reportage" such as modern biography might be.

Again, a third gain one would achieve is that the canonical Gospels would likewise no longer be seen as having emerged in a cultural vacuum but as having resulted from the Christian appropriation of a genre that was already in use in contemporary culture. Indeed, the real question scholars must attend to, it would seem, is not whether the Gospels have affinity to ancient Greco-Roman biography but what the exact dimensions of this affinity are.[37]

When all is said and done, what one would like to think is the chief gain to be achieved in having the canonical Gospels commonly acknowledged as being of the nature of ancient biography is that this would enable one to interpret them better as to their "meaning" and "purpose." But although there are those who claim that better interpretation necessarily results from such acknowledgment, the fact of the matter is that this seems to be only marginally true. To begin with, works belonging to the same genre are each, in certain respects, peculiar; the peculiarity of a work, however, plays no small role in determining its meaning. Then, too, the same genre can, in principle, be employed for more than one purpose. In view of these two considerations alone, it becomes apparent that whatever "meaning" and "purpose" scholars may ascribe to a genre as a whole will apply only in a general way to any work belonging to that genre. To say, for instance, that the purpose of Matthew is to present Jesus as the crucified and risen Messiah and to inspire emulation of him and faith in him is to make a statement that is so broad in scope that it tells one little unless it is elaborated at considerable length.

The Redaction-Critical Approach

It was noted above that a major scholarly preoccupation of the nineteenth and early twentieth centuries was the quest of the historical Jesus. Because there were some few scholars who held that Matthew and not Mark was the first Gospel to have been written, Matthew, too, was used to accomplish the objectives of the quest. Matthew, too, was therefore thought by some to be of the nature of biography understood in a modern vein as historical reportage.

At the turn of the century, Johannes Weiss[38] and Albert Schweitzer[39] sounded the death knell of the liberal quest of the historical Jesus. By the same token, the single most important factor in overcoming the historical-biographical approach to Matthew's Gospel was the rise of NT form criticism following World War I. Redaction criticism, which emerged as a distinct discipline following World War II, was in many respects an extension of form criticism.

One of the principal contributions of the form critics was that they called attention to the importance of the "situation in life" *(Sitz im Leben)* in the preservation and development of the gospel tradition. Subsequently, scholars have learned to distinguish broadly between three such life situations.

The first situation in life has to do with the times of the earthly Jesus. Surrounded by his disciples, Jesus in the course of his ministry proclaimed the nearness of the kingdom of God, preached his message also in parables, instructed his disciples, performed miracles, engaged in debate with the leaders of the Jews, sat at table with toll collectors and sinners, and went the way of the cross. To attempt to determine and to understand what Jesus said or did or what happened to him on any given occasion of his ministry is to attempt to place a word of his or a story about him in its first situation in life.

The second situation in life pertains to the years immediately following Easter when the church came into being and, in the expectation of Jesus' imminent return, proclaimed him to the Jews and then to the gentiles as the Christ crucified and raised. There is no evidence that Jesus ever left behind a written document. This means that in the aftermath of Easter it was up to the followers of Jesus to recall words he had spoken, deeds he had done, or events they knew had happened to him (e.g., his baptism, temptation, or transfiguration). What kind of words, deeds, or events did they recall, and to what end? To judge from the Gospels, the followers of Jesus recalled sayings and parables of his in which they knew him to be revealing his divine authority, or setting forth his message of the kingdom, or sketching the ethics of the kingdom, or describing the way of discipleship, or teaching his disciples to pray, or telling of things to come. As for his deeds, they recalled miracles he had performed, debates he had had, or other events that revolved around him.

What motivated the followers of Jesus to recall such sayings, deeds, and events? As a result of the Easter appearances of Jesus, his followers believed him to be alive and exalted by God to rulership. They understood him to be present in the circle of their community, presiding over it in the power of his Spirit. Accordingly, through the recollection of sayings of his and narratives about him they knew him to be interacting with them in their worship and guiding them in their preaching, teaching, life, and controversies with opponents. The vehicles for such remembering were quite simply "mind and mouth." Therefore the words of Jesus and the narratives about him, the "stuff" that makes up the written Gospels, can be seen to have assumed the form of an oral tradition. Then, too, since Jesus was indeed confessed to be alive, his followers furthermore believed that he spoke to them, not only through the recollection of past words and deeds, but also afresh: through new or adapted words for new and changed situations.[40] Thus, from its inception the gospel tradition was not static but dynamic in character, for through it the living and reigning Christ was seen as communicating with his followers in ever different circumstances. To attempt to determine the form and meaning of a saying of Jesus or narrative about him in relation to the setting in which it was used in the worship, life, and mission of the early church following Easter is to attempt to place that saying or narrative in its second situation in life.

The third situation in life is associated with the age of the evangelists. Following Easter, the gospel tradition was, as mentioned, oral in form. At this stage, sayings and parables of Jesus and stories about him circulated among Christians independently of one another. In point of fact, long after certain portions of the gospel tradition had been committed to writing, other portions continued to be transmitted from one generation to another by word of mouth. Still, after a period of years the time came when a written tradition did begin to emerge. Although it is a debated issue, some scholars believe that the gospel-source dubbed "Q" is an example of an early, written document.[41] It appears to have been a collection of sayings of Jesus interspersed with several narratives, dating from about A.D. 45 or 50. An unusual feature is that it seems not to have contained a passion narrative.

However one is to think of Q, the first written document that may be called a "Gospel" in the literary sense of the term was most likely Mark (c. A.D. 70).[42] Matthew and Luke followed some years later (c. A.D. 85 or 90), and John was written last, at the end of the first century.

Redaction critics have directed their attention to the Gospels themselves and to the Christian communities in which they arose. As regards Matthew, Mark, and Luke, the so-called synoptics, painstaking scrutiny reveals basic similarities and differences among them, both as to makeup and wording. From what one can tell, each evangelist, in response to the peculiar needs and situation of his church, has presented Jesus and his ministry in his own unique way. Although none of them has approached his subject matter as a modern-day novelist but has instead bound himself in large measure to gospel traditions handed down to him, all nevertheless must be respected as genuine authors. On this point, redaction critics have taken issue with their form-critical predecessors: whereas the early form critics regarded the evangelists as mere editors, transmitters, or compilers of the gospel tradition, redaction critics speak of them as "author personalities," as individuals who have worked creatively with the gospel materials at their disposal. At any rate, to attempt to determine the exact character, purpose, and message of any given Gospel with a view to the historical situation that gave rise to it is to attempt to analyze that Gospel in relation to the third situation in life.

One more word concerning the rise of redaction criticism is in order. Although redaction criticism did not attain the status of an independent discipline until after World War II, one should not imagine that there were not scholars between the wars whose work did not anticipate this approach to Matthew. In terms of the way Matthew has been interpreted, a continuum runs from the era of form criticism to that of redaction criticism.

A Comparison with Literary Criticism

Since World War II, redaction criticism has unquestionably been the dominant method of research in the field of Gospel studies. Recently, however, literary criticism has come to the fore. How do the two methods compare with each other?

In its most commonly practiced form, literary criticism focuses on the Gospel of Matthew as narrative.[43] A "narrative" is composed of a story and its discourse.[44] A "story" is made up of settings, characters, and events that comprise the plot. In the case of Matthew, the story is of the life of Jesus from conception and birth to death and resurrection. The "discourse" is the means whereby a story is put across. In the case of Matthew, it encompasses the kind and style of language that is used, including the many rhetorical devices. It also encompasses such matters as the "implied author" who stands behind the whole of the story, the "narrator" (i.e., the "voice") who tells the story, the "implied reader" who understands and appropriately responds to the story, and the various aspects of "point of view" (evaluative, phraseological, psychological, and spatial and temporal) which the narrator or any given character may adopt in the course of the story. So construed, a narrative like that of Matthew constitutes a "world" that is peopled by characters and governed by its own ordinances.

Accordingly, the emphasis in literary criticism is on approaching Matthew's Gospel as a narrative that creates a "world" of its own which the reader is invited to enter, to dwell in for a time, and then to leave again. By contrast, the emphasis in redaction criticism is on approaching Matthew's Gospel as a literary document that is the sum of layers of tradition which extend from the evangelist himself all the way back to the earthly

Jesus. In literary criticism, the reader dwells in the autonomous world of the narrative. In redaction criticism, the reader enters a stream of tradition that began with Jesus and has flowed through the early church and down to the evangelist.

Since the focus in literary criticism is on the unity of the text and in redaction criticism on the text as the sum of layers of tradition, the two methods are at greatest remove from each other in those studies where the redaction critic places the stress on disassembling the text so as to separate tradition from redaction. By the same token, in those studies where the redaction critic engages in what is known as composition criticism and concentrates on the wholeness of the text, the two methods approach each other and can even overlap. The stress in this present study is on the wholeness of Matthew; technically, it is a study in composition criticism.

To illustrate the similarities and differences between literary criticism and that form of redaction criticism known as composition criticism, consider the following representative examples. In composition criticism, the "author" of the First Gospel is termed Matthew and is conceived of as a flesh-and-blood Christian who was living around A.D. 85 and was a member of the church for which he was writing. In literary criticism, the author generally referred to is the so-called implied author. The implied author, however, is the author as he or she can be known from reading the text. So understood, the implied author cannot in reality be identified with any flesh-and-blood person but is a construct of the text. In composition criticism, the "reader" of the First Gospel is conceived of as any real person ever involved in the process of hearing it or reading it. The obligation of the reader, however, is to identify himself or herself as closely as possible with the members of that church of first-century Christians on behalf of whom Matthew wrote and at whom Matthew aimed the message of his Gospel. In literary criticism, the reader usually referred to is the so-called implied reader. The implied reader is no actual person of any century but is an imaginary person who understands the text perfectly and responds to it appropriately. In other words, the implied reader, too, is a construct of the text. And last, in composition criticism, the "world" of the First Gospel denotes the actual circumstances—social, religious, political—which prevailed at the time Matthew wrote and in which he and the members of his church were living. In literary criticism, the Gospel's "world" denotes that autonomous world created by the narrative which is, strictly speaking, not inhabited by any "real" human being but by the characters of the story. The "real reader" visits this world and, in so doing, may gain a new perspective with which to view the "real world" in which he or she actually lives.

From these three illustrations, one gets some idea of how distinct the two methods of literary criticism and composition criticism are. But such distinctness notwithstanding, the two methods can also be found, in the study of the thought of Matthew, to lead to many conclusions that are either the same or compatible.

Attempts at Defining the Nature and Purpose of Matthew

Matthew's Gospel is not, it was argued above, of the nature of biography, construed as historical reportage, the purpose of which is to repristinate for future generations the life and times of Jesus. Similarly, correct as it may well be to say that Matthew's Gospel is of the nature of ancient biography, it is not immediately apparent how this insight can be turned to advantage for achieving a significantly better understanding of the Gospel. This leads one to ask: How have those who have taken some form of redaction-critical approach to the First Gospel assessed its nature and purpose?

A close look at the First Gospel reveals the fivefold use in it of the following stereotyped formula: "And it happened when Jesus finished . . ." (7:28; 11:1; 13:53; 19:1; 26:1). This formula marks the conclusion of five great speeches of Jesus and thus calls attention to them: the Sermon on the Mount (chaps. 5—7), the missionary discourse (chap. 10), the parable discourse (chap. 13), the ecclesiological discourse (chap. 18), and the eschatological discourse (chaps. 24—25). Furthermore, it is also striking that Matthew should describe Jesus, in connection with his giving his first discourse, as ascending the "mountain" to deliver it. In view of these factors, could it not be that the First Gospel is of the nature of a compend of Jesus' commandments arranged after the fashion of the Mosaic Pentateuch for the purpose of combating within Matthew's church the heresy of lawlessness?[45] Or contrariwise, could it not be that the Gospel is of the nature of a Book of Origin that has the character of a "shattered Pentateuch"? If so, should its purpose not be construed as conveying to Matthean Christians the self-understanding that they are the community of Jesus, the New Human Being, who has inaugurated a new humankind?[46]

The schematic way in which Matthew has arranged his Gospel is apparent throughout. Might not the arrangement of the Gospel therefore indicate that it is of the nature of a lectionary[47] or catechism,[48] the purpose of which is, respectively, to provide scripture readings for the church's services of worship or instruction for Christian converts?

In addition to the careful way in which the First Gospel has been composed, a consideration of matters of content that are most typically Matthean reveals an emphasis on a broad range of subjects: ethics, apostleship, teaching about the kingdom, church discipline, and eschatology. Is it not compelling, then, to regard Matthew's Gospel as of the nature of a manual, the product of a school, the purpose of which is to aid teachers and church leaders in instruction and administration within the church?[49]

From another perspective, Matthew lends great prominence in the opening verse of his Gospel to the word "book." On the assumption that this word describes the entire document Matthew has written, must not his Gospel be held to be of the nature of a "book" the purpose of which is to highlight "sermons"[50] or the "new verbal revelation"[51] which Jesus mediates to his church?

The First Gospel reveals that Matthew has also reflected in depth on questions relating to the history of salvation. For example, one problem of great concern to him was the relationship of the church to Israel. In recognition of this, is not the Gospel to be thought of as being of the nature of a revised version of Mark, the purpose of which is to portray the church as the "true Israel" which has replaced the Jews, or "false Israel," who have forfeited their place in the history of salvation as God's chosen people?[52] Or, in variation of this, is not the Gospel to be regarded as being of the nature of historical reflection standing in the service of preaching, the purpose of which is to counter doubt that God keeps his promises by asserting that he has in fact been faithful to his people throughout history and that in Jesus and in the church his promises are coming to fulfillment?[53]

But scrutiny of the First Gospel reveals that the place of the law in the church was likewise of central concern to Matthew. Should this be true, is not the Gospel to be looked upon as being of the nature of a legal document, the purpose of which is to exhort the followers of Jesus in the time of the church to observe Jesus' normative interpretation of God's will over against both Pharisaic Judaism and Hellenistic antinomianism?[54]

Again, Matthew lived at a time that seems no longer to expect the imminent return of Jesus. Does not this suggest that he has composed a "life of Jesus" with eschatological relevance and ordered it as the "way of righteousness" in the ongoing history of salvation?[55] Or what of the themes of the gentile mission or of the persecution of Christians, which also stand out so noticeably in the First Gospel? Is not the First Gospel to be seen as being of the nature of a "life of Jesus" and "Acts of the Apostles" rolled into one, the purpose of which is to set forth the more recent history of salvation: the "pre-history of the Messiah," the "history of the call of Israel," and the "call of the gentiles"?[56] Or is it not rather to be seen as a document the composition of which has been governed by the experience of Matthew's church of internal dissension and of external opposition from the gentile nations?[57]

Still, true as these points may be, perhaps one does best to construe the situation in life in which the First Gospel arose in a yet broader sense and recognize that Matthew's church was a church in transition: a once strongly Jewish-Christian community was becoming increasingly gentile in its makeup. This shift in constituency called for a reinterpretation of past traditions. Is it not the case, therefore, that the First Gospel constitutes a "remodeling" of the Christian message as contained in such sources as Mark and Q? And would its purpose not therefore be to set forth a new vision of the history of salvation according to which Jesus' death-resurrection is viewed as the apocalyptic turning point that brings to a close the sacred past of Jesus' own life and ushers in a new epoch, the time of the church?[58]

None of these redaction-critical attempts to specify the nature and the purpose of Matthew's Gospel can be lightly dismissed. All of them underline basic aspects of the Gospel which must be explained if the document and the context in which it emerged are to be understood. Most immediately, however, the value of these attempts is that they stress the necessity of beginning an investigation of the Gospel by considering matters relating to its composition.

Questions Concerning the Composition of Matthew

An important question in dealing with the composition of the First Gospel is whether Matthew the author is to be identified with Matthew the apostle (9:9; 10:3). In chapter 4, the authorship of the Gospel will be discussed in greater detail. But here it must be said that the evidence does not seem to indicate that Matthew the apostle was the author of the Gospel. For one thing, Matthew the author appears to have set Mark's Gospel at the basis of his work. According to one count, he has appropriated more than 600 of the 661 verses of Mark's text.[59] What is more, it also appears that he has followed the outline of the Second Gospel.[60] Broadly speaking, in both of them Jesus discharges his ministry in Galilee, undertakes the journey to Jerusalem, and there suffers and is raised. If Matthew the apostle were Matthew the author, such dependence upon Mark, whom no one claims was an apostle or eyewitness of Jesus, is virtually inexplicable. Why did the apostle Matthew not draw from his own recollection of events? Hence, it is highly doubtful that Matthew the author should be identified with Matthew the apostle and thought of as an eyewitness to the events of the ministry of Jesus.

Some commentators have attempted to circumvent this conclusion by suggesting that Matthew the apostle influenced the final shape of the First Gospel in the sense that he was the author of the sayings-source Q or of a primitive Aramaic document that was translated into Greek and incorporated into canonical Matthew. But against the latter thesis stands the fact that canonical Matthew cannot be described as translation Greek. And whether Matthew the apostle had anything to do with Q is a moot point, since we are without means either to prove this assertion or to disprove it.

In view of the shape of the First Gospel, what prompted Matthew to revise Mark? The answer is that Mark was no longer adequate to meet the needs of Matthew's church. This can be seen especially well in the areas of Christology, ecclesiology, and the history of salvation.

Thus, Mark presents Jesus above all as the Son of God who refers to himself in the course of his ministry as the Son of man. Matthew follows suit, but develops both categories more extensively. He also stresses to a greater degree than Mark the notion that Jesus Messiah, the Son of God, is the exclusive teacher of his church.[61] In other respects, Matthew furthermore transforms Mark's isolated references to Jesus as the Son of David[62] into a major christological category that he employs not only descriptively, in relation to the person of Jesus, but also polemically, against Israel. And whereas Mark makes no great use of the term *kyrios* ("Lord") as applied to Jesus,[63] Matthew utilizes it numerous times in order to underline his exalted station and divine authority. Along these same lines, Matthew also heightens the majesty of Jesus' person by eliminating a number of Marcan references to his "feelings," namely, that he was "angry" (Mark 3:5), was "moved with pity" (Mark 1:41), "wondered" (Mark 6:6), "sighed deeply in his spirit" (Mark 8:12), "became indignant" (Mark 10:14), or looked upon a man and "loved" him (Mark 10:21). Finally, Matthew also attributes to Jesus designations not found in Mark, such as "Emmanuel" (1:23), "servant" (12:18), and "Son of Abraham" (1:1).

Ecclesiologically, Mark gives the impression that the Christians of his community were free from the Jewish law and the Pharisaic traditions surrounding it (Mark 7:1–23). Matthew, by contrast, was writing in a situation in which Jewish and Jewish-Christian influence was most pronounced, as chapter 4 will show. Positively, he advocates the abiding validity of the law as Jesus has interpreted it, and stresses in addition, on the part of the disciples, the greater righteousness (5:17–20). Negatively, Matthew's community, although suffering tribulation at the hands of gentiles (24:9; 10:22), was experiencing even greater persecution at the hands of Jews.[64] Moreover, it was also beset internally by severe moral and spiritual aberrations (24:10–12). In the face of such problems, Matthew exhorts his fellow Christians on a broader scale than Mark to single-hearted devotion to God (5:48) and loving concern for the "brother" (chap. 18), threatening them with judgment and promising them eschatological reward.[65]

As for the history of salvation, it is generally held that Mark was written at about A.D. 70, close to the fall of Jerusalem. Matthew, on the other hand, was removed from this event by a number of years. In reflecting on the history of salvation, he tends to "periodize" more than Mark. For one thing, he formally extends this history backwards to Abraham, and treats the "time of Israel (OT)" as a distinct time of prophecy. By the same token, he introduces the so-called formula quotations into his text and hence stresses in a special way the "time of Jesus" as the time of eschatological fulfillment.[66] Even the "time of Jesus" is divided into discernible periods: the ministry of John (3:1–2), of Jesus (4:17), of the disciples (10:5–7), and of the post-Easter church (24:14; 26:13), to the end of the age. By setting off the time of Jesus from the "time of Israel (OT)" and by dividing the time of Jesus into segments, Matthew is able to call attention in remarkably clear fashion to the time of Jesus as the age of salvation, to the person of Jesus as the basis of salvation, and to the post-Easter task of the church, the community of disciples of Jesus. In all of the above ways— christologically, ecclesiologically, and in terms of the history of salvation—Matthew shows that he found it necessary to revise Mark's Gospel.

If Matthew revised Mark's Gospel, by what means did he do so? In all, the First Gospel comprises some 1068 verses. More than 600 of these can, as was noted, be traced to Mark, about 235 to Q, and the rest have come from oral or written traditions peculiar to Matthew himself. Now since Matthew did not for the most part compose freely but took over these traditions of the sayings of Jesus and of the narratives about him, it is obvious that he did not enjoy unrestricted freedom in composing a document that would "speak" to the church of his day. To write of the past in a way that would meet the needs of the present, Matthew made use of a number of literary devices that enabled him to interpret traditional materials by carefully editing them. What are some of these literary devices?

To begin with, Matthew arranges his sources in such a way as to *expand* upon the outline of Mark. Such expansion can be found at the beginning and end of the Gospel, within the body of the Gospel, and even within individual pericopes. To the story of John the Baptist, for instance, Matthew affixes a genealogy (1:2–17) and a cycle of infancy narratives (1:18—2:23). Whereas Mark has one resurrection narrative, Matthew has four (28:1–8, 9–10, 11–15, 16–20). Within the Gospel, the great speeches of Jesus represent in large measure Q and special material which Matthew has gathered together to form huge blocks of sayings or parables and fitted into the Marcan outline at prescribed points.[67] The formula quotations of the OT provide examples of how Matthew can introduce material into single pericopes.[68]

Some few additions in the Gospel appear to have been composed by Matthew himself. It may be that he was drawing upon older traditions which he either completely rewrote or first committed to writing. In any event, a minute analysis of the style, vocabulary, and contents of the pericopes on the origin of Jesus (1:18–25), Jesus' discussion with John (3:14–15), and the great commission (28:16–20), to cite but these, make it almost certain that these stem from the hand of Matthew himself.

In the second place, Matthew *rearranges* his sources. This has already been observed with respect to Q: Matthew groups the sayings of Jesus in this source to form great speeches.[69] As for Mark, Matthew follows him with considerable fidelity throughout the last half of the Gospel (13:53—28:8), but in the first half establishes a different sequence of events both by expanding upon Mark's outline and by transposing several Marcan pericopes to a new position.[70]

Again, Matthew *abridges* his sources. Perhaps the best example of this is the manner in which he redacts the miracle stories of Mark. Take the healings of Jairus's daughter and the woman with the hemorrhage. Mark's account covers twenty-three verses (5:21–43). Matthew's account requires but nine (9:18–26). While retaining the words of Jesus, Matthew has dropped a large amount of narrative. The result is that under the pen of Matthew the two stories have become highly compact scenes depicting in dramatic fashion the encounter between Jesus, in whom God's power inheres, and persons in desperate need.

Fourth, Matthew *clarifies* his sources. Often this has to do with matters of style, as when Matthew changes Mark's awkward expression "those who were about him with the twelve" (4:10) to "the disciples" (13:10). But at times it is more far-reaching than this. Consider again the story of the woman with a hemorrhage. As Mark tells it, the woman comes up behind Jesus in the crowd and touches his garment (5:27). The sudden release of healing power seems to occur of itself (5:29–31). Only after the miracle has already taken place does Jesus sanction it (5:34). In Matthew's version, all this has changed. As soon as the woman touches Jesus' garment, he turns around and confronts her (9:22). Not until after he has explicitly sanctioned the healing does it take place (9:22d). By editing the story in this fashion, Matthew shows that he is concerned that the reader labor under no false illusions: Jesus is most assuredly in complete control of all events surrounding the miracle; nothing happens without his knowledge or consent.

Last, Matthew *omits* material from his sources or *substitutes* one piece of tradition for another. An example of omission can be seen in the fact that Matthew has taken over the verses that both precede and follow Mark 3:20–21, but not these. The reason is not hard to find: the notion that the relatives of Jesus should think him "mad" does not comply with Matthew's exalted understanding of his person. An example of substitution can be found in chapter 13: Matthew has appropriated the whole of Mark 4 with the single exception that one finds the parable of the tares (13:24–30) where one should expect to find the parable of the seed growing secretly (Mark 4:26–29).

Consequently, one sees from the First Gospel that Matthew has received traditional materials and interpreted them by redacting them, through expansion, rearrangement, abridgment, clarification, omission, and substitution. The end result is that he has created a new literary document which narrates the gospel-story afresh to meet the needs of the church to which he belonged. And because Matthew did present his church with a new version of the gospel-story, a consideration of the composition of the Gospel calls for comment yet on his use of characters, of settings, and of the summary passage.

The characters of the Gospel tend to play fixed roles. Jesus is the protagonist, the "hero" of the story. Angels are supernatural beings whose presence signals, or alludes to, the immediate or future intervention of God in human affairs, often on behalf of Jesus (cf. chaps. 1—2; 28). Satan is likewise a supernatural being, the transcendent adversary of Jesus. The disciples are the followers of Jesus: they are both "with him," as when they obey him and function as eye- and ear-witnesses to his ministry, and "against him," as when they refuse to hear of his death and resist the notion of discipleship understood as servanthood (16:21–28; 20:20–28). The many little people who come to Jesus for help or healing or who otherwise serve him exemplify true faith or service. The Jewish crowds form the background for much of Jesus' activity in public, but they remain unbelieving and in the passion narrative join their leaders in condemning Jesus to death. The Jewish leaders of whatever designation are the inveterate opponents of Jesus. Now as the reader works his or her way through the gospel-story, his or her attitudes about what is right or wrong, true or false, are shaped by Jesus and the comments Matthew himself makes. In learning of Jesus, the reader learns of the basis of salvation. In observing Jesus in interaction with other characters, the reader will draw close to or distance himself or herself from these other characters and so learn, either positively or by reverse example, what it means to be a follower of Jesus in post-Easter times.

Of the settings in which Jesus is described as carrying out his ministry, only a select number are of more than literal significance. For example, "Galilee" is the place where Jesus proffers salvation to Israel (4:12, 23) and where his church following Easter begins its mission of salvation to the gentiles (28:16–20). The "desert" is both a place where end-time expectation comes to fulfillment (3:1) and the abode of Satan (4:1). The "mountain" is a place where one is near to God, where eschatological teaching and revelation take place, and where Jesus stands forth as the Son of God.[71] The "sea" is a place of fear and great danger (8:23–27, 32; 14:23–33). "Capernaum" and "Nazareth," the two cities in which Jesus is at home in Galilee (2:23; 4:13), are symbols of the rejection of divine grace (11:23–24; 13:54–58). "Jerusalem" is the place where Jesus must die (16:21). It is the "home" of such as are his mortal enemies: Herod (chap. 2), Pilate (chap. 27), and the "chief priests and the elders of the people."[72] The "temple," as the dwelling place of God, is depicted as having been superseded through death and resurrection by the person of Jesus Son of God (26:61; 27:51). And in chapter 24, the phrase "in those days" connotes the "last times" that will culminate in Jesus' visible return in glory for judgment.

As for the summary passage, Matthew deftly employs it in order to alert the reader to the direction that the plot of the gospel-story will take. Two sets of three summary passages each dominate the greater part of the Gospel. In 4:17–16:20, the passages are 4:23; 9:35; and 11:1. They describe Jesus as discharging throughout the whole of Galilee a ministry of teaching, preaching, and healing whereby he proffers salvation to Israel (4:17–11:1). Israel, however, responds to Jesus' ministry by repudiating him (11:2–16:20), and the gravest sign of this is that the Jewish leaders take counsel on how to destroy him (12:14). This, in turn, sets the tone for the three summary passages that govern the final third of the Gospel: the passion predictions (16:21; 17:22–23; 20:17–19). These predictions repeatedly remind the reader that the gospel-story is moving inexorably toward one, divinely appointed outcome: the cross and resurrection.

Thus, the redaction critical approach to Matthew's Gospel focuses above all on its composition. What kind of document is it? What is its intention? How does the story develop? How have the sources been shaped? What is the nature of the church that stands behind it? In what manner of historical situation was it written, and does it reflect this situation? And what, in view of these queries, is its message? The task is to address these issues in the course of this book, and to begin by sketching the composition-critical approach that will control the discussion.

A Redaction-Critical Approach in Outline

The question still being pursued is that of the nature and purpose of Matthew's Gospel. Generally overlooked is the circumstance that Matthew himself suggests how they are to be defined. He does this with the expression he has coined, "the gospel of the kingdom" (4:23; 9:35; 24:14; 26:13).

It should be observed that Matthew does not distinguish, as the present-day historian must, between the message *of* Jesus to Israel and the post-Easter message of the church *about* Jesus. Instead, he designates both as "the [this] gospel of the kingdom." In 4:23 and 9:35, for instance, Matthew describes Jesus Messiah, declared by God at his baptism to be his unique Son (3:17), as going around all Galilee proclaiming to Israel "the gospel of the kingdom." Similarly, he records in 24:14 and 26:13 that what the disciples, or church, of Jesus will proclaim in all the inhabited world is "this gospel of the kingdom." Whether it is preached as "testimony" to Israel or to the gentiles, this gospel, which may also be termed "the word of the kingdom" (13:19), effects for the hearer salvation or damnation.[73]

Although Matthew utilizes this one expression to designate both the preaching of the earthly Jesus and that of the post-Easter church, surprisingly he nowhere explains in a sentence what it means. How, then, is it to be understood? To ascertain this, the constituent terms "gospel" and "kingdom" must be examined.

The stem *euaggel-* is at the basis of the Greek words for "gospel" *(euaggelion)* and "to proclaim (announce) news" *(euaggelizomai)*. Whether or not the earthly Jesus ever employed these or equivalent terms in connection with his proclamation of the message of the kingdom of God is difficult to know. But for his part, Matthew was heir to Q and Mark. Q, it appears, arose in a Jewish-Christian community that sprang up in the first years following the resurrection and maintained itself in a Palestinian environment. In this community, the verb "to announce news" referred in all likelihood to a preaching of the coming in the near future of Jesus in his role as the Son of man.[74]

Whereas Matthew found the verb "to announce news" in Q, he appropriated the noun "gospel" from Mark. In Mark, this word is indissolubly joined to the person of Jesus as the Messiah Son of God. The emphasis is not solely on Jesus' parousia,[75] but also on his ministry, death, and resurrection. Indeed, "gospel" in Mark is definite and most often absolute in character ("the gospel"),[76] and denotes the proclamation of God's decisive act of salvation on behalf of humankind in Jesus Messiah, the Son of God, above all in his death and resurrection.[77]

Matthew, then, brings together in his Gospel the Q tradition, which contains the verb *euaggelizomai* (meaning "to announce the imminent coming of Jesus in his role as the Son of man"), and the Marcan tradition, which highlights the noun *to euaggelion* (meaning "the gospel [Jesus Messiah, the Son of God]"). Since he employs the verb only once (cf. the Q logion 11:5) but makes prominent use of the noun (4:23; 9:35; 24:14; 26:13), it is plain that it is the latter that is of special importance.

Now the expression "the [this] gospel of the kingdom" in Matthean thought is thoroughly christological in coloration. It may not seem so at first glance, because it reads "the gospel *of the kingdom*." Still, in 4:23 and 9:35 it refers to the message that specifically Jesus Messiah, the Son of God, proclaims. And in 26:13, "this gospel," which denotes the message the disciples are to proclaim throughout the whole world, includes also mention of the woman's act of pouring oil on the head of Jesus (26:6–13). In other words, in these three passages there is solid evidence that in the church of Matthew the term "gospel" encompassed at once traditions of sayings of Jesus and traditions of narratives about him. In view of this, the term "gospel" in the expression "the gospel of the kingdom" may be defined as the news about the kingdom, which saves or condemns, which is revealed in and through Jesus Messiah, the Son of God, and is announced first to Israel and then to the gentiles.

What is the meaning of the term "kingdom"? To begin with, the absolute designation "the kingdom" is simply an abbreviation of the fuller idiom "the kingdom of heaven." Although statistics reveal that Matthew prefers the latter to "the kingdom of God," the two expressions are synonymous. Because the genitive "(of) heaven" is subjective in nuance and a metonym for "God," the purpose of the expression "the kingdom of heaven" is to assert the truth that "God rules (reigns)." Hence, "the rule of God," or "the reign of God," is a proper paraphrase of it.

The notation in 4:23 and 9:35 that Jesus goes about Galilee proclaiming the gospel of the kingdom calls to mind the passages 3:2; 4:17; and 10:7, where Matthew pictures John the Baptist, Jesus, and the disciples as all announcing that "the kingdom of heaven is at hand *(ēggiken)*." The Greek verb *ēggiken* in these summary statements denotes a "coming near," an "approaching," that is spatial or temporal in character. In light of this, it becomes evident that what Matthew depicts John, Jesus, and the twelve as proclaiming to Israel is that the rule of God has drawn near. Thus, one recognizes that if the term "gospel" in the Matthean expression "the gospel of the kingdom" finds its center in the person of Jesus Messiah, the Son of God, the term "kingdom" finds its center in the person of God. At the same time, even the term "kingdom" in the First Gospel is not without a christological focus, for Matthew states in words of the OT in 1:23 that it is in the son born to the virgin that God draws near to dwell with his people. In line with these emphases, therefore, the entire expression "the gospel of the kingdom" may be explicated as follows: it is the news that saves or condemns which is revealed in and through Jesus Messiah, the Son of God, and is proclaimed first to Israel and then to the gentiles to the effect that in him the eschatological rule of God has drawn near to humankind.

With this definition in mind, an attempt can at last be made to define the nature and the purpose of the First Gospel. It was mentioned above that Matthew nowhere explicitly informs the reader how he or she is to understand the expression "the gospel of the kingdom." Instead, he simply assumes that when he uses it, the reader or hearer will know what is meant. On what grounds was he able to make this assumption? He could do so on the grounds that the reader or hearer would have access to the document he had written. Accordingly, although Matthew does not employ the expression "the gospel of the kingdom" to denote a written document per se, in the final analysis it is the contents of his document—the words of Jesus and the narratives about him—that elucidate this expression. Once this is clear, it likewise becomes clear that the document Matthew has written is in fact of the nature of a "gospel." This document conveys, as has been observed, the news revealed in and through Jesus Messiah, the Son of God, and so it may be termed a "kerygmatic story." Hence, the grand conclusion one arrives at is that *Matthew's document is of the nature of a "gospel," that is to say, a kerygmatic story. Its purpose is, again, to announce the news that saves or condemns which is revealed in and through Jesus Messiah, the Son of God, and is proclaimed first to Israel and then to the gentiles to the effect that in him the eschatological rule of God has drawn near to humankind.*

A look at the two chief structural features of the Gospel corroborates this understanding of its nature and purpose. These two features are (a) the topical outline according to which the contents of the Gospel are arranged, and (b) the view of the history of salvation the Gospel projects.

To take first the topical outline,[78] at 4:17 and 16:21 Matthew employs the following formula: "From that time on Jesus [Christ] began to. . . ." This formula signals the beginning of a new phase in the life and ministry of

Jesus. In addition, each of the verses in which the formula is embedded stands apart to a degree from its context and sounds the theme that Matthew subsequently develops throughout a larger portion of his Gospel. Hence, if one construes these verses, and 1:1 as well, as "headings" and presses them thematically, this topical outline readily emerges: (I) The Person of Jesus Messiah (1:1—4:16); (II) The Public Proclamation of Jesus Messiah (4:17—16:20); and (III) The Suffering, Death, and Resurrection of Jesus Messiah (16:21—28:20).

How, specifically, does this topical outline undergird what has been said of the nature and purpose of the Gospel? The grand conclusion reached is that Matthew's Gospel is of the nature of a kerygmatic story the purpose of which is to announce news that tells of the revelation God makes known in and through Jesus Messiah, his Son. The topical outline confirms the truth of this conclusion both by indicating how the term "kerygmatic story" is to be understood and by culminating in each of its three main parts in a scene that portrays Jesus precisely as the Messiah, the Son of God.

As to how to understand the term "kerygmatic story," the topical outline shows that Matthew's Gospel assumes the contours of a "life of Jesus." This "story" of the life of Jesus is "kerygmatic" in the sense that it tells of the person of Jesus,[79] of his ministry of teaching, preaching, and healing and of Israel's repudiation of him,[80] and of his suffering, death, and resurrection.[81]

As for the scenes in which the three main parts of the topical outline culminate, in all of them Jesus is portrayed as the Messiah, the Son of God. Thus, at the baptism God himself declares over Jesus and in the hearing of the world of transcendent beings such as Satan that Jesus is his unique Son (3:13–17; cf. 4:3, 6). At Caesarea Philippi, Peter declares on behalf of the disciples that Jesus is the Messiah, the Son of the living God (16:13–20). And at the Great Commission, the exalted Jesus, to whom God has entrusted all authority in heaven and on earth, refers to himself as "the Son" (28:16–20), which is but one indication that he stands before his disciples and commissions them in his capacity as the resurrected Messiah, the Son of God.[82] This special stress on Son-of-God Christology in the three main parts of Matthew's topical outline reveals that this outline substantiates what was said of the nature and purpose of the Gospel by singling out Jesus Messiah, the Son of God, in his person and in his public activity and in his death and resurrection, as the "place" where God encounters people with his eschatological rule.

The second chief structural feature of the Gospel that corroborates the understanding of its nature and purpose as defined above is Matthew's concept of the history of salvation. The so-called formula quotations,[83] which are peculiar to this Gospel, indicate in broad lines how this concept is to be defined. In these passages, a quotation of the OT is introduced by words that emphasize its "fulfillment" in some phase of the life of Jesus. Structurally, therefore, these passages show that Matthew makes a basic distinction between the "time of Israel (OT)" as the time of prophecy and the "time of Jesus" as the time of fulfillment. Because Matthew traces the genealogy of Jesus back to Abraham (1:1, 17), it is plain that he conceives of the "time of Israel (OT)" as having begun with him.

Fundamentally, then, Matthew differentiates between two epochs: the "time of Jesus (earthly—exalted)" and the "time of Israel (OT)." Within the overarching time of Jesus, however, he also develops, as was seen, a sequence of temporal subcategories: there is the ministry to Israel of John (3:1-2), of Jesus,[84] and of the disciples (10:5-7), and the ministry to the nations of the post-Easter church.[85] Because Matthew "periodizes" in this manner, it should be observed that he does not operate with a "time of the church" which stands apart from the time of Jesus. In Matthew's concept of the history of salvation, the so-called time of the church, Matthew's own time, is characterized by the ministry to the nations which the post-Easter disciples carry out in the final period of the time of Jesus under the guidance of the exalted Son of God.

Now it will be recalled that the First Gospel was described, in the definition given above of its nature and purpose, as being a kerygmatic story that conveys the news, which saves or condemns, that is proclaimed first to Israel and then to the gentiles. By the same token, Matthew also depicts, in his concept of the history of salvation, the "time of Jesus (earthly—exalted)" as embracing the ministries to Israel of John (3:1-2), of the earthly Jesus (4:17; 15:24), and of the disciples (10:5-7), and the ministry to the nations of the post-Easter church (24:14; 28:19-20). In Matthew's scheme of things, therefore, Israel has been decisively confronted with the news that saves or condemns, and this news is furthermore being proclaimed to the gentiles. Accordingly, Matthew's concept of the history of salvation substantiates what was said of the nature and purpose of the Gospel in that it reveals that God's activity in his Son is of ultimate significance for Israel and the gentiles alike.

Thus far in the discussion, the nature and purpose of the First Gospel have been defined and its two chief structural features, the topical outline and the concept of the history of salvation, have been treated. One thing yet remains: to specify the central thought that controls the Gospel.

The central thought that controls the Gospel comes to the fore in the passages 1:23 and 28:20, which form a bracket around the Gospel and hence constitute what is known as an "inclusion." These passages, and 18:20 as well, express the thought that *in the person of Jesus Messiah, his Son, God has come to dwell to the end of time with his people, the church, thus inaugurating the eschatological age of salvation.* If one gives careful consideration to this thought, one will recognize that it encapsulates everything that has been said to this point about the nature and purpose of the Gospel and about its topical outline and concept of salvation history. This thought is the one that controls Matthew's Gospel.

Of great importance is the fact that in this central thought the theology, Christology, and ecclesiology of Matthew can be seen to converge. On the one hand, the notion that "God is present with his eschatological rule in the person of Jesus" describes the relationship Matthew establishes between theology and Christology, between God the Father and his Son Jesus (cf. also 11:25–27; 28:18). On the other hand, the notion that "God in the person of Jesus is with us" is Matthew's own description of the relationship he establishes between Christology and ecclesiology, between Christ and his church (1:23; 28:20; also 18:20). The factor that ties these statements together is of course "Jesus," which means that Matthew's Gospel is essentially christological in orientation: it is only by attending to Jesus Messiah, the Son of God, that one comes to know who God is and what the church is.

In view of all this, the further task to be accomplished is now clear: to treat in terms of the central thought of the Gospel Matthew's understanding of the figure of Jesus (chap. 2), of the kingdom of heaven (chap. 3), and of the community of the disciples (chap. 4). In the concluding portion of chapter 4, the situation of Matthew will also be discussed.

CHAPTER TWO

MATTHEW'S UNDERSTANDING
OF JESUS

The central thought controlling the First Gospel is, as was noted last chapter, that in the person of Jesus Messiah, his Son, God has drawn near to dwell to the end of time with his people, the church, thus inaugurating the eschatological age of salvation (1:23; 18:20; 28:20). In this chapter and the next, the ramifications of particularly the first part of this central thought will be explored: that it is in the person of Jesus Messiah, his Son, that God is present among humankind. The specific focus of this chapter will be on the Christology of Matthew, or better, on Matthew's portrait of Jesus. And since the Gospel's topical outline shows that Matthew has organized his materials to describe, in turn, the person of Jesus Messiah (1:1—4:16), his public ministry and repudiation (4:17—16:20), and his journey to Jerusalem and death and resurrection (16:21—28:20), it is by looking to this outline and especially the first part that one discovers the heart of Matthew's portrait of Jesus.

The opinion is sometimes expressed that the best way to proceed in treating the Christology of the evangelists is to strive to capture the overall picture each one sketches in place of analyzing individual titles such as "Messiah," "King of the Jews," "Son of David," "Son of God," and so on. In the case of Matthew, however, the analysis of titles is indispensable on two counts: the various titles function in recognizable ways; and the relationships among them have been carefully drawn. Then, too, the precision and sophistication Matthew displays in working with titles should dispel at last the erroneous notion that his portrait of Jesus is primitive and underdeveloped.[1] The truth of the matter is that Matthew has reflected in depth on the figure of Jesus and has fashioned a sharply etched profile of him.

The designation for Jesus that Matthew uses more often than any other is, in fact, "Jesus." "Jesus" in the First Gospel has the status of a personal name. This is evident from the related circumstances that Matthew lists the son born to Mary in his genealogical table as "Jesus" (1:16) and also has Joseph, on divine command, legally give him this name (1:21, 25).

Another indication that Matthew regards "Jesus" as a personal name is the fact that although the Gospel is not, as was seen, rich in biographical detail, what there is seems to be clustered around "Jesus." Thus, the one Matthew calls "Jesus" is portrayed as born in "Bethlehem" (2:1, 5–6) and raised in "Nazareth."[2] He is the "son of the carpenter," and his mother's name is, again, "Mary" (13:55). He has both "sisters" and "brothers," the names of the latter being "James," "Joseph," "Simon," and "Judas" (13:55–56). As an adult, he moves from Nazareth to "Capernaum" (4:13), which is known as "his own city" (9:1), where he apparently has a "house."[3] In Jerusalem to the south, he can be recognized, as can also his disciples, as one who comes "from Galilee" (26:69, 73; also 21:11).

On the other hand, there is one passage in which the designation "Jesus" occurs which stands apart from the others: 1:21. Because "Jesus" means in essence "savior" ("God is salvation") and Matthew in 1:21 plays on this meaning ("You shall call his name 'Jesus,' for he shall *save* his people from their sins"), the impression one gets is that "Jesus" has ceased to be a mere personal name in this passage and become instead a title of majesty. But this impression is mistaken. For Matthew, "Jesus" remains the personal name of the man from Nazareth. Christologically, the claim Matthew raises on behalf of the man "Jesus" is that he is the Son of God. By the same token, the mission God entrusts Jesus Son of God is to accomplish salvation from sins (cf. 26:28 with 27:38–54). The reason Matthew plays on the meaning of the name "Jesus" in 1:21 is to highlight this mission of accomplishing salvation from sins that Jesus will carry out. But this notwithstanding, the character of the designation "Jesus" as a personal name in the First Gospel is unmistakable.

Jesus as Messiah

The term "Messiah," or "Christ" *(christos)*, is one of the first titles the earliest church ever applied to Jesus (cf. Acts 2:36). It was not long before it also became a personal name, often used in association with "Jesus" ("Jesus Christ").[4] For his part, Matthew employs the term both ways. Thus, in 1:1, 18; and 16:21, "Jesus Christ" is plainly a name, although in 1:18 the correct reading of the text is probably "Christ" and in 16:21 "Jesus." Even as a personal name, however, "Jesus Christ" conveys for Matthew the underlying truth that Jesus, born of Mary, is the Messiah, God's Anointed.[5]

While in the OT it is the high priest and especially kings who are said to be the anointed of God,[6] prophets, too, could be so designated.[7] Since in three places in the First Gospel Jesus is called "prophet," the question is whether Matthew views it as a title of majesty.

The answer is unequivocally negative. For Matthew, "prophet" is the term that properly applies to OT figures such as Isaiah[8] or Jeremiah,[9] or even to a circle of Christians within his own church (cf. 10:41; 23:34). But this is the extent of it. Even in relation to John the Baptist, "prophet" proves to be an inadequate designation because it connotes too little. Thus, the unbelieving Israelite "crowds" think of John as a prophet (14:5; 21:26). But Jesus declares to them that he is "more than a prophet" (11:7, 9). He is, in reality, the forerunner of the Messiah (11:10).

These same "crowds," or "men," also view Jesus as a prophet.[10] But to a yet greater degree than in the case of John, this is to see in him too little: such a "confession" implies no personal commitment to Jesus but only contrasts the populace with their leaders. The leaders are unable to honor Jesus even as a prophet because they hold him to be a false messiah who is in collusion with the prince of demons.[11] Consequently, the true perception of Jesus from Matthew's standpoint is not that he be regarded as a prophet but, as Peter confesses on behalf of the disciples by revelation of God, as the Messiah, the Son of God (cf. 16:14 with 16:16). Once this is clear, it further becomes clear that Jesus' statement in Nazareth that "a prophet is not without honor except in his own country and in his own house" (13:57) is best interpreted along the following lines: Jesus' former neighbors, like his worst enemies and unlike even the crowds, will not afford him so much as the honor due a prophet.

Accordingly, the term "prophet" is not a title of majesty in the First Gospel, and Matthew does not cast Jesus in the role of "Prophet-Messiah." How, then, does Matthew understand the title "Messiah"?

In Matthew's scheme of things, the Messiah, that is, the Coming One foretold by the prophets and awaited by Israel (11:2–6), is a kingly figure. He is, to be sure, Jesus,[12] who stands in the royal line of David[13] and brings the history of Israel to its culmination (1:1, 17). Invested with the authority of God, he means salvation or damnation for people.[14]

This is Matthew's initial description of Jesus as the Messiah. Throughout his Gospel he develops it further, mainly in terms of two other titles. The first of these is the "King of the Jews [Israel]."

When Matthew relates the title "Messiah" to the "King of the Jews

[Israel]," it assumes, from the vantage point of the characters in the gospel-story, political overtones that are uniformly negative. The only group of characters for whom this does not hold true is the Magi. They come to Jerusalem to worship the newborn King of the Jews (2:2). But as for others, Herod, because he fears the loss of his throne, plots to kill the Messiah, the King of the Jews (2:2, 4, 13, 16). Elsewhere, Pilate and the Roman cohort accede to the charge that "Jesus . . . the King of the Jews . . . who is called the Messiah" is a political throne-pretender.[15] And in that the leaders of the people mock the crucified Messiah as the "King of the Jews" (27:37), they are pictured as taking up where the Romans have left off: Jesus, placed by the Romans on the cross as the "King of the Jews" (27:35–37), does not even have at his command sufficient power to get himself down and so prove this messianic "claim" for which he is being executed.[16]

The preceding are examples of what may be designated as the "public" conception of Jesus as the Messiah: such figures in the gospel-story as Herod and Pilate attempt to deal with Jesus the Messiah as though he were claiming for himself politically the throne of Israel. In stark contrast to this is Matthew's positive, or "confessional," description of Jesus as the Messiah. According to it, Jesus Messiah is depicted as the King who suffers on behalf of his people. By defining the kingship of Jesus Messiah in this way, Matthew effectively disabuses the reader of the Gospel of any notion that Jesus was the insurrectionist his enemies made him out to be.

To illustrate this, when Jesus enters Jerusalem as the Son of David, Matthew inserts into his Marcan text a formula quotation that refers to him as the "humble King" (21:5). This reference points ahead to chapter 27, which tells of the suffering Jesus endures as King at the hands of Pilate and on the cross. In the pericope 27:27–31, Matthew provides a detailed sketch of the true nature of Jesus' kingship: as he stands draped in a scarlet robe with a crown of thorns on his head and a reed for a scepter in his right hand, the soldiers abuse him and, kneeling in mock obeisance before him, hail him as "King of the Jews." Hence, if "King" characterizes Jesus Messiah as a political throne-pretender in the eyes of his enemies, in the eyes of Matthew it characterizes him as the one in the line of David[17] who establishes his rule, not by bringing his people to heel, but by suffering on their behalf.

In Matthew's perspective, therefore, Jesus as the Messiah is not a prophetic but a royal figure. He comes from the house of David, and the entire history of Israel culminates in him; indeed, he means salvation or damnation for people. As the "King of the Jews [Israel]," the "public" conception of him is that he is a political throne-pretender. In reality, however, he is the King of his people in the sense that he suffers on their behalf.

Earlier it was said that Matthew develops "Messiah" in terms of two titles of majesty. If the one title is the "King of the Jews [Israel]," the second one is the "Son of God." Furthermore, a glance at chapter 27 shows that in the story of Jesus on the cross (27:38–54), where the suffering of Jesus on behalf of others reaches its climax, the title "King of Israel" gives way to the title "Son of God" (cf. 27:40, 43, 54). What this means, as will be discovered shortly, is that Matthew's view of Jesus as Messiah-King is taken up into his more expansive view of Jesus as the Son of God. It is this title that lies at the heart of Matthew's portrait of Jesus.

Jesus Messiah, the Son of God

It has been said repeatedly that Matthew devotes the first main part of his topical outline to the person of Jesus Messiah (1:1—4:16). Here he sets forth his fundamental understanding of Jesus. To get at this, the first main part must be examined according to structure and content.

Because the genealogy and infancy narratives with which Matthew's Gospel begins are followed in chapter 3 by the public ministry of John the Baptist, the prevailing opinion among scholars is that chapters 1—2 stand apart from the rest of the Gospel and should be construed as its prologue. Still, a careful study of 1:1—4:16 reveals that it deserves to be regarded as the first larger section of the Gospel. Four factors indicate this.

The first factor is the presence in the Greek text at 3:1 of the particle *de* ("now," "then"). The context reveals that Matthew frequently employs this particle in the opening line of a pericope in order to connect that pericope with preceding narrative (cf., e.g., 1:18; 2:1, 13, 19; 4:12). By employing *de* at 3:1, Matthew shows that the interpreter is not to posit a fundamental break between chapters 2 and 3 but, on the contrary, is to view the pericopes of the two chapters as in some sense belonging together.

A second structural indication that the pericopes comprising chapters 1—2 and 3:1—4:16 are to be thought of as a single larger section is the formula quotations in 2:23 and 4:12-16. It is generally held that the travels of Jesus prior to his public ministry come to an end when Joseph brings Mary

and the infant Jesus from Egypt and settles in Nazareth (2:23). But a look
at these formula quotations proves that these prior travels of Jesus do not
in reality end until he takes up residence in Capernaum. It is to make this
point that Matthew shapes the passage 4:12–14 in such a way that it takes
up flawlessly on the previous passage 2:22–23. These passages read as follows: ". . . *he* [Joseph, with Mary and the infant Jesus] *went and dwelt in
a city called Nazareth,* that what was spoken by the prophets might be fulfilled . . ."; ". . . *he* [Jesus] *left Nazareth and went and dwelt in Capernaum*
by the sea, in the regions of Zebulun and Naphtali, that what was spoken
by the prophet Isaiah might be fulfilled. . . ."

This mention of the travels of Jesus prior to his public ministry calls
attention to yet a third indication of the unity of 1:1—4:16: all of the
pericopes in this larger section narrate events that are *preliminary* to Jesus'
ministry to Israel. When Jesus does finally appear openly in Israel, Matthew marks this with summary passages (4:17, 23–25; 9:35; 11:1). But
earlier, Jesus is pictured as leading a "private" existence, and there are
only signs that he is about to undertake a public ministry. When John, for
example, carries out his ministry to Israel (3:1–12), Jesus is not present, so
that John foretells his coming (3:11–12). When John baptizes Jesus, he is
the sole witness present, for no reference is made to the crowds or to the
Israelite leaders (3:5–7). The force of the adverb "then" *(tote)* at 3:13 is
that it removes chronologically and temporally the baptism of Jesus from
previous events (cf. "then," also at 4:1).

All of the pericopes that make up 1:1—4:16, therefore, have this "preliminary quality" about them. In addition, all of them can likewise be shown
to stand in the service of one dominant motif. This is a fourth indication
of the unity of 1:1—4:16. What this motif is comes to the fore in the series
of related idioms with which Matthew punctuates the entire section: "his
people" (1:21), "my people" (2:6), "my Son" (2:15; 3:17), and "the Son
of God" (4:3, 6). In other words, the motif of the divine sonship of Jesus
Messiah runs like a red thread through 1:1—4:16, so that this larger section
reveals itself, not only structurally but also materially, to be, again, the first
main part of the Gospel.

Now if one accepts 1:1—4:16 as the first main part of Matthew's Gospel
and also keeps in mind the related idioms just cited, one arrives easily at
Matthew's understanding of Jesus. In a sentence, Matthew presents Jesus,
the Messiah-King from the line of David and of Abraham, as the royal Son
of God.

In the opening verse of the Gospel, Matthew describes Jesus Messiah as the "Son of David" and the "Son of Abraham." Jesus is the Son of David because Joseph son of David, on divine command, gives him his name, adopting him into his line (1:20, 25). Jesus is the Son of Abraham, for the entire history of Israel, which bears promise also for the gentiles, reaches its culmination in him (1:17; 8:11). Still, although it is not said in 1:1 because the genealogy with which Matthew begins extends to Abraham and not God (cf. Luke 3:38), Jesus is preeminently the "Son of God."

As early as 1:16, Matthew alludes to the divine sonship of Jesus Messiah. He casts the verb *gennaō* in the passive voice, in this way alerting the reader to special activity on the part of God ("Jesus *was born* [by a miraculous act of God]"). This verb, in turn, points forward, to the passive participle *gennēthen* ("that which *is conceived*") in 1:20, which also alludes to divine activity. This participle is found in the pericope on the origin of Jesus (1:18–25). In this pericope, Matthew records, respectively, that Mary's conception was "by the Holy Spirit" (1:18, 20), that God through the prophet disclosed the true significance of the person of her son ("God with us," 1:22–23), that Mary was a "virgin" when she bore him (1:23), and that the child could not have been from Joseph because Joseph made no attempt to have relations with Mary until after she had given birth to her son (1:25). When all these terms and statements are conjoined with one another, their overall intention is clear: they affirm that Jesus Messiah, born of Mary, is nevertheless the Son of God, for his origin is in God.

In chapter 2, Matthew continues his presentation of the person of Jesus Messiah. The Magi arrive in Jerusalem and ask where the newborn "King of the Jews" is to be found (2:2). Herod responds by designating this king as the "Messiah" (2:4), the one whom he anticipates will lay political claim to his throne, as is obvious from his secret desire to destroy Jesus (2:13). Against Herod's faulty notion of the Messiah, the Israelite leaders, quoting from scripture, unwittingly advance a correct understanding of him: in reality, the Messiah is the long-promised shepherd, or eschatological king, of God's people Israel (2:5b–6).

Now it is highly significant that, following 2:6, Matthew never once refers to Jesus in chapter 2 as "king" or "ruler," but instead refers to him consistently as "the child" and repeatedly employs the expression "the child and [with] his mother" (cf. 2:8–9, 11, 13–14, 20–21). The remarkable thing about this latter expression is that it is at once appropriate to the narrative and a means whereby Matthew can speak of Jesus without giving the impression that he is the son of Joseph and hence exclusively the Son of David (1:20, 25). Thus, it becomes plain that the purpose of the expression "the child and [with] his mother" is to remind the reader that the son of Mary is at the same time the Son of God. Consequently, the term "the child" in chapter 2 reveals itself to be a surrogate for "Son of God." Indeed, Matthew himself confirms this observation: at 2:15, which is a formula quotation, he breaks his otherwise consistent use throughout 2:7–23 of the expression "the child and [with] his mother" so that none other than God, through the prophet, might call "the child" Jesus "my Son." In the last analysis, therefore, one sees that "the child" whom the Magi come to Bethlehem to "worship" (2:11) as the "King of the Jews" is in fact the "Son of God," just as "the child" whom Herod plots to kill is no political throne-pretender but the eschatological shepherd of God's people who is likewise the "Son of God."

To move quickly to the pericope on John the Baptist (3:1–12), Matthew depicts John as referring to Jesus as the "Coming, mightier One" whose appearance is imminent and will result in salvation or damnation for Israel (3:11–12). This reference creates anticipation in the mind of the reader for the arrival of Jesus at his baptism.

The pericope on the baptism (3:13–17) is crucial to the portrait of Jesus that Matthew develops in 1:1—4:16 and contains several emphases. For one thing, Jesus does not submit to baptism by John either because he, like Israel, has need to repent of sin[18] or because he would become a disciple of John. On the contrary, he submits to baptism because, as he himself asserts, it is God's will that he and John should "fulfill all righteousness" (3:15). In brief, Jesus submits to baptism by John according to Matthew because God wills it and Jesus renders to God perfect obedience.

The occurrence of the words "and behold" at 3:16b and 3:17a calls attention to the fact that it is in these verses, especially the latter, that the story of the baptism culminates. The purpose of the opening of the heavens is both to permit the Spirit to descend and to signal that divine revelation is about to take place (cf. Ezek. 1:1). The descent of the Spirit upon Jesus attests to the divine act whereby God empowers him to discharge the messianic ministry he is shortly to begin (4:17). Such "empowerment," of course, is not to be interpreted as Jesus' initial endowment with the Spirit, for he was conceived by the Spirit. Instead, it is a commentary on what it meant for John to designate Jesus as the "mightier One" (3:11). The words of the voice from heaven, "This is my beloved Son, with whom I am well pleased" (3:17), declare Jesus, this Messiah-King from the line of David, to be God's only, or unique, Son whom God has chosen to be the bearer of his eschatological rule.[19]

In the declaration of the heavenly voice at 3:17, one reaches the apex, not only of the story of the baptism, but also of the entire first part of Matthew's Gospel (1:1—4:16). In this part, Matthew describes the person and origin of Jesus. The overriding truth he promulgates is that Jesus—who is Messiah, King of the Jews, Son of David, and Son of Abraham—is the royal Son of God. In 1:1, the heading of the first part of the Gospel, Matthew makes no mention of the divine sonship of Jesus. His reason for this is twofold: first, the genealogy with which he begins does not, as was mentioned, extend to God but only to Abraham; and second, Matthew intends that Jesus' divine sonship, as something that can be known solely by revelation (11:27; 16:16-17), be first proclaimed, not by any character in the gospel-story and not even by himself as narrator, but only by God. Accordingly, Matthew alludes to this truth with circumlocutions,[20] with metaphors,[21] or with a term ("son") that is susceptible to dual meaning,[22] and he even permits it to sound softly as the word of the Lord spoken through the prophet (1:22-23; 2:15). Still, all remains adumbration until that climactic point following the baptism of Jesus when the voice from heaven proclaims over Jesus and in the hearing of the world of transcendent beings such as Satan that Jesus is indeed the unique Son of God (3:17; 4:3, 6).

The pericope on the temptation (4:1-11) flows from the climactic verse 3:17 even as the previous pericopes have tended toward it. It develops in particular one aspect of the divine sonship of Jesus, namely, his perfect obedience to the will of God. As one belonging to the world of transcendent beings, Satan was privy to God's declaration that Jesus is his Son. Accordingly, three times Satan puts Jesus to the test in Jesus' capacity as the Son of God. In that these testings are antitypical to those experienced by Israel, who was also God's son (Exod. 4:22-23), in its wanderings from Egypt to Canaan, Jesus recapitulates this history of Israel. But whereas Israel son of God broke faith with God, Jesus Son of God renders to him perfect obedience.

The pericope 4:12-16 is transitional in nature. Its purpose is to place Jesus, whom Matthew has presented in full as Messiah Son of God, in "his own city" of Capernaum in Galilee, where he will begin his public ministry to Israel.

In light of the preceding discussion, the series of related idioms referred to above can again be cited—"his people" (1:21), "my people" (2:6), "my Son" (2:15; 3:17), and "the Son of God" (4:3, 6)—and the contents of the passages in which they occur summarized. Taken together, these passages provide a concise sketch of the overall portrait of Jesus that Matthew draws in the first part of his Gospel. This sketch is the following: Jesus Messiah, in the line of David (1:21), is the Son of God (2:15; 3:17); that is to say, he has his origin in God (1:20) and is the one chosen to shepherd the eschatological people of God (2:6). Empowered by God for messianic ministry (3:16-17), he proves himself in confrontation with Satan to be perfectly obedient to the will of God (4:1-11). As such a one, he saves his (God's) people from their sins (1:21).

The Son of God as One Who Teaches, Preaches, and Heals

Matthew begins his Gospel by identifying Jesus Messiah above all as the Son of God, which means in a nutshell that in him God has drawn near with his eschatological rule to dwell with his people (1:23). The second and third main parts of the Gospel have to do with the public ministry of Jesus Messiah (4:17—16:20) and with his suffering, death, and resurrection (16:21—28:20). What kind of activity does the Messiah Son of God undertake in Israel? To know this is to comprehend better Matthew's portrait of him.

Before specific aspects of the activity of Jesus are examined, mention must first be made of facets of Jesus' divine sonship not yet treated. From all that has been said, it should be obvious that, in Matthew's eyes, Jesus is the Son of God in a manner that can be predicated to no other human being. For example, through Jesus the disciples enter into fellowship with God and hence become "sons of God,"[23] but he alone is the "Son of God." For this reason, Jesus speaks of God in the First Gospel as "my Father"[24] or, with an eye to the disciples, as "your Father,"[25] but never as "our Father." The Lord's Prayer is no exception to this, because "our Father" (6:9) is the address the disciples as a group are to use in their approach to God.

Since Jesus is uniquely the Son of God, the relationship he has with God is unique. This is implied already by his conception through the Holy Spirit (1:18, 20) and by his empowerment with the Spirit following his baptism (3:16). But it is in the pericope on Jesus' thanksgiving to the Father (11:25–27) that this is most emphatically brought out. In this pericope Jesus Messiah, "the Son," both addresses God as "Father" and employs the absolute expression "the Father." The unique relationship between the Son and the Father is characterized by the verb "to know" (*epignōskō*; v. 27). This verb connotes total unity of will between the Father and the Son, and what this means is that, on the one hand, the Father elects the Son and authorizes him to represent him in the world and, on the other, that the Son acknowledges this election by living in complete fellowship with the Father, giving to him perfect obedience. In addition, because the Son and the Father "know" each other, it is the Son who alone "reveals" the Father to people, through all he says and all he does, that is, through his messianic ministry (11:27, 2–6).

In consequence of the unique relationship that exists between Jesus Messiah, the Son of God, and God his Father, the Father entrusts the Son with divine authority (*exousia*). The upshot is that what the Son says and does is said and done on the authority of God. God himself is fully active in the messianic ministry of his Son.

Matthew never tires of making this point. Often he does so obliquely, but in select passages he does so explicitly. In the Sermon on the Mount, for example, it is as one invested with divine authority that the Matthean Jesus declares: "You have heard that it was said to the men of old . . . but I say to you. . . ."[26] At the conclusion of this sermon, Matthew writes: "The crowds were astonished at his teaching, for he taught them as one who had authority . . ." (7:28–29). In 11:27, Jesus Messiah exclaims: "All things have been given over to me by my Father. . . ." In the pericope on the question about authority (21:23–27), the thrust of Jesus' argument is that just as John the Baptist carried out his ministry on the authority of God, so he, the Son of God, wields in the house of God through teaching (21:23) and healing (21:14) the authority of God. In 28:18, the exalted Son of God asserts: "All authority in heaven and on earth has been given to me." Finally, in one passage Jesus claims divine authority for himself, not as the Son of God, but as the Son of man (9:6). This ostensible anomaly will be explained below.

Jesus Messiah, then, is the divine Son who speaks and acts on the authority of God, his Father. In describing the messianic activity of Jesus in Israel, Matthew states that he "teaches," "preaches," and "heals" (4:23; 9:35; 11:1). What is the significance of these terms?

The Preaching of Jesus

The verb "to preach" *(kēryssō)* may be considered first, since it is used less frequently than the others. If one asks whom Matthew reports as "preaching," it is first of all John the Baptist. John proclaims repentance in view of the nearness of the kingdom of heaven (3:1-2), and the focus of his proclamation is on Jesus, the "Coming, mightier One" whose appearance means salvation or damnation for people (3:11-12). Next, Jesus himself is said to preach, and his proclamation, like that of John, announces repentance in view of the nearness of the kingdom of heaven.[27] The heart of his message, as was noted, is that in his own person and work God's eschatological rule is a present reality. Third, the disciples of Jesus are likewise enjoined to preach, and they, too, announce the nearness of the kingdom (10:7). Their preaching is an extension of Jesus' ministry. Hence, their message has the same content as his. Last, mention is also made that the church following Easter will preach (24:14; 26:13). Once again, the focus of this message is on the person and work of Jesus.

What this survey shows is that the function of the verb "to preach" in the First Gospel is to establish continuity of ministry and message among John, Jesus, the disciples, and the post-Easter church. In other words, Matthew utilizes this verb to inform the reader that throughout the entire "time of Jesus (earthly—exalted)," which extends from his birth to his parousia, and therefore throughout the successive ministries of John, of the earthly Jesus, of the disciples, and of the post-Easter church, the message of the kingdom, which finds its center in God's activity in Jesus Messiah, the Son of God, has been, is being, and will be, proclaimed. Accordingly, Matthew draws on this verb to assert to the members of his church that Jesus preached the gospel of the kingdom (4:23; 9:35) and that they preach the gospel of the kingdom (24:14; 26:13). Matthew's purpose is to make them aware that "now," just as "then," it is the proclamation of this message that results in the salvation or condemnation of people.

Because the verb "to preach" in the First Gospel stresses continuity of ministry and message as regards John, Jesus, the disciples, and the church, it is not singularly indicative of the activity of Jesus. It would not be in keeping with Matthew's thinking, therefore, to describe Jesus as the "Preacher." Strictly speaking, he is not a preacher in a way others are not.

The Teaching of Jesus

Of the three verbs with which Matthew describes the activity of the Messiah Son of God in Israel, the verb "to teach" *(didaskō)* in 4:23; 9:35; and 11:1 has the position of stress. This indicates that Matthew attaches special importance to it. If Matthew would not call Jesus the "Preacher," would he call him the "Teacher"?

The answer is decidedly negative if this means that "teacher" is to be construed as a title of majesty. In chapter 1, the point was made that Matthew, unlike Mark, never permits the disciples to address Jesus with the synonymous terms of "rabbi" or "teacher," but only the traitor Judas (26:25, 49) and such strangers or opponents as a "scribe" (8:19), "some of the scribes and Pharisees" (12:38), the rich "young man" (19:16, 22), the "disciples" of the Pharisees and the "Herodians" (22:16), the "Sadducees" (22:23–24), and a "lawyer" who tempts him (22:36). The disciples, by contrast, consistently address Jesus as "Lord." In only one place does Jesus instruct the disciples to refer to him as "teacher" (26:18), and this is in connection with a conversation they are to have with a stranger in which "teacher" expresses the way in which this man will regard Jesus (26:17–19). Thus, as far as Matthew is concerned, "rabbi" and "teacher" are terms of human respect. As the proverb 10:24 puts it, they denote the kind of respect a disciple owes his mentor or a slave his master.

Consequently, "teacher" in the First Gospel is not a title of majesty but a public term of human respect by which Matthew pictures strangers and opponents of Jesus as approaching him as though he were no more than one Jewish rabbi among others. But in what manner, then, does Matthew characterize Jesus in those scenes in which he pictures him as delivering authoritative instruction to the disciples, or church? Matthew gives us the answer in 23:8–10: it is Jesus the "Messiah" who is the one teacher of the disciples. But on this view, how would Matthew have the reader understand his use here of the title "Messiah"? From previous discussion, from Peter's confession in 16:16, and from the question of the high priest in 26:63, it is clear that the one teacher of the disciples, or church, is Jesus Messiah, the Son of God. But should this be correct, why does Matthew not make use of the title Son of God in 23:8–10?

This has to do with the nature of this title. In 16:17, Matthew says in a logion of Jesus that it is only by divine revelation that any human being can penetrate the mystery of his person and know him to be the Messiah Son of God. Those who utter the title Son of God apart from divine revelation do so in ignorance of its true meaning and hence make themselves guilty of blasphemy and mockery (cf. 26:63-66; 27:39-43). In Matthew's eyes, therefore, "Son of God" is not a "public" title, for Jesus is not recognized in public to be the Son of God. But in 23:1, Matthew records that it is in the company of the "crowds" as well as the disciples that Jesus speaks the words of 23:8-10. The answer, therefore, is that Matthew does not use the title Son of God in 23:8-10 because the very setting he has established precludes for him the use of it. In any event, the statement stands: the one teacher of the disciples, or church, is Jesus Messiah, the Son of God.

In setting forth the teaching activity of the Messiah Son of God, Matthew emphasizes one factor in particular: he makes known the will of God in terms of its original intention. For Matthew, the Son of God is the mouthpiece of God in a direct and immediate fashion. In a variety of ways Matthew calls attention to this. Thus, he remarks that Jesus teaches with an authority not found among the scribes, and depicts the crowds as being astonished by it (7:28-29). Indeed, Jesus teaches in a way that makes him the supreme interpreter of the law. His word is more radical than that of Moses and can even stand above it.[28] In disputes between Jesus and the Israelite leaders over matters of law, Matthew, in comparison for instance with Mark, prefers to stress the fact that Jesus speaks the mind not merely of Moses but, more importantly, of God.

The three examples of the latter are worthy of note. In debate with the "Pharisees and scribes" over the law and the tradition of the elders, Matthew does not, like Mark, have Jesus introduce his quotation of the law with the words "for *Moses* said . . ." (Mark 7:10), but with the words "For *God* said . . ." (15:4). Again, in debate with the "Pharisees" on divorce Matthew redacts Mark's pericope in order to emphasize more strongly than the latter the supersession of the will of Moses by the will of God.[29] Last, in debate with the "Sadducees" over the question of the resurrection, Matthew emends Mark's version of the words of Jesus (". . . have you not read *in the book of Moses* . . . how *God* said to him . . ."; Mark 12:26) to read: ". . . have you not read what was said to you by *God* . . ." (22:31), thus eliminating a reference to Moses and making the reference to God stand out more starkly.

That Jesus Messiah, the Son of God, should be seen as the supreme arbiter of the will of God is of the greatest significance to Matthew both theologically and practically. His church is, as will be seen in chapters 3 and 4, embroiled in conflict with contemporary Pharisaic Judaism. Both sides acknowledge the law as the expression of the will of God. But each side interprets it quite differently. From the standpoint of Matthew's church, the interpretation that Pharisaic Judaism gives the law results in the perversion of God's will. Through the authoritative teaching of Jesus, however, the will of God has truly been revealed and the law properly interpreted.

This explains two phenomena one finds in the First Gospel. Positively, the Matthean Jesus designates the response he calls upon his disciples to make to his teaching of the law and of the will of God as the righteousness that is "greater" than that of the "scribes and Pharisees" (5:20). Negatively, the Matthean Jesus excoriates the Israelite leaders for their understanding and practice of the law. They are "hypocrites," for their works are evil.[30] They are "blind guides" who lead people to destruction.[31] While concerning themselves with trivial matters, they neglect the weightier matters of the law: justice, mercy, and faithfulness (23:23). For the sake of their tradition of the elders, they transgress the law of God (15:3). In short, they fail to perceive that the deepest intention of God's law is not "sacrifice" but "mercy," or love.[32]

Because Jesus Messiah, the Son of God, stands forth as the supreme arbiter of the will of God, Matthew stresses throughout his Gospel the permanently binding character of his teaching. This, finally, is the reason Matthew highlights the teaching of Jesus to the extent he does: it reveals the will of God for all time to come. As far as the activity of "preaching" goes, Jesus engages in this, but so do John, the disciples, and the post-Easter church. But in the case of "teaching," Jesus alone is the one who does this. So it is that Matthew never even intimates that John or the pre-Easter disciples "teach," and when the exalted Son of God commissions his church to go to the nations, it is no accident that what these followers are given to "teach" is "all that *I* have commanded you" (28:20). For Matthew, Jesus Messiah, the Son of God, is in truth the one teacher of his church.

Thus far, no mention has been made of the parables of Jesus. In Mark, three references to teaching introduce the so-called parable chapter (4:1–2). Although 13:1–52, the Matthean counterpart to Mark 4, contains some eight parables of Jesus,[33] Matthew studiously avoids suggesting that they represent "teaching" on the part of Jesus.[34] Why is this?

Matthew states in words of Jesus in the pericope on the reason for speaking in parables (13:10–17) that the Israelite crowds are unable to comprehend the parabolic speech of Jesus because they are blind, deaf, and without understanding. In line with this statement, therefore, Matthew does not characterize the parabolic speech of Jesus to the crowds as "teaching" because it constitutes an apology before Israel.

The Healing of Jesus

The third verb with which Matthew describes the public activity of Jesus in the summary passages 4:23 and 9:35 (cf. 11:5) is "to heal" *(therapeuō)*. Just as Jesus is not "Teacher" or "Preacher" in the First Gospel in the sense that these terms are titles of majesty, so neither is he "Healer." To Matthew's way of thinking, the one who "teaches," "preaches," and "heals" with divine authority is, again, Jesus Messiah, the Son of God.

What is the significance in the First Gospel of the healing, or, to put the question more broadly, of the miraculous activity of the Son of God?[35] With other biblical writers, Matthew shares the view that disease in people or upheaval in nature are symptoms of sin and of bondage to Satan. This is why there is a close relationship also in the First Gospel between "faith" and the "forgiveness of sins" on the one hand and healing and the calming of storms on the other.[36] This is furthermore why the Matthean Jesus boldly declares in one verse: "But if it is by the Spirit of God that I cast out demons, then the kingdom of God has come upon you" (12:28). Through the activity of healing no less than through the activity of teaching and preaching, Matthew portrays Jesus as calling Israel to repentance and as liberating people from the sphere of Satan's rule and bringing them into the gracious sphere of the rule of God (11:20; 12:28). In one passage, Matthew follows Mark in depicting the exorcisms of Jesus as a "plundering" of the kingdom of Satan.[37]

It is important to observe how Matthew does not use miracle stories. He does not use them, for example, to "prove" the divine sonship of Jesus. To Matthew, miracles are incapable of providing proof such as this. Twice in the Gospel he records that Jesus, having cast out a demon, is immediately accused by the Pharisees as having accomplished this, not by the power of God, but by the power of the prince of demons (9:34; 12:24). Or one may look at it this way: had Matthew thought that miracles were capable of proving the divine sonship of Jesus, surely he would not have recounted the two stories that tell how the Israelite leaders witness miracles of Jesus only to ask him for a sign that will yet convince them that he is God's emissary to Israel.[38]

It was just said that the broad significance of the miracle story is that it portrays Jesus as bringing to bear upon the ills of people and the disturbances in nature the gracious, saving power of God's eschatological rule. In chapters 8—9, Matthew demonstrates best the role that the miracle story (where it does not function as supportive scenery for a debate or to teach the disciples of the power of faith) plays in the Gospel. In these chapters, Matthew gathers together a series of ten miracle stories, edits them so as to place the accent on the direct speech between Jesus and his partners in dialogue, and embeds them in a framework that has to do mainly with the theme of "following" Jesus.[39] These factors suggest that Matthew places the miracle story in the service of his concept of discipleship, and the reason he does so is to make it relevant for the members of his church.

Thus, for Matthew's church Jesus is the exalted Son of God and no longer the earthly Son of God. With divine authority, the earthly Son of God performed mighty "acts of power" *(dynameis)*.[40] Similarly, the exalted Son of God, who resides in the midst of his church and to whom God has given all authority in heaven and on earth,[41] can perform mighty "acts of power." He does so, and this is Matthew's argument in chapters 8—9, on behalf of the disciple in post-Easter times who approaches him worshipfully and prayerfully in the attitude of trust even as the characters in these miracle stories are pictured as approaching him with their prayer-like requests in the attitude of trust. To put it succinctly, Matthew employs the miracle story in chapters 8—9 to teach the members of his church that Jesus Messiah, the exalted Son of God, is ever near them with his saving power.

In respect to the overall flow of Matthew's gospel-story, it should be noted in passing that, following 11:1, when Jesus becomes the rejected Messiah of Israel, Matthew continues to describe him as healing people in Israel, even great numbers.[42] Through his ministry of healing to Israel, Jesus Son of God shows that he is indeed Israel's Messiah despite the fact that his preaching and teaching have fallen on obdurate hearts.

A final matter begs for consideration. Why is it that Matthew has Jesus deliver his first major sermon (chaps. 5—7), which is the example par excellence of his teaching, in the setting of the mountain (5:1)? Luke, by contrast, identifies the plain as the place where it is given (6:17). And, what is particularly striking, why does Matthew select exactly the mountain as the setting for Jesus' mass healing of people (15:29–31)? Practically speaking, what could be more inconsiderate than that the "many crowds" coming to Jesus should be required to lead or carry up the mountain "the lame, the maimed, the blind, the dumb, and many others" to place them at the feet of Jesus (15:30)?

The answer, of course, has nothing to do with logistics but with theology. A survey of the Gospel reveals that the only title of majesty Matthew associates with the setting of the mountain is the "Son of God."[43] Owing to its height, the mountain readily connotes nearness to God and hence is a place where prayer and divine revelation take place. In the First Gospel, this setting also alludes to Jesus as the Son of God. Thus, in that Jesus "teaches" and "heals" the crowds from atop the "mountain," he is revealing himself to be Israel's Messiah, the Son of God, the one who speaks and acts in the stead of God.

The Mission of the Son of God

The second and third main parts of the topical outline of Matthew's Gospel have to do with the public ministry of Jesus Messiah to Israel and Israel's repudiation of him (4:17—16:20) and with his journey to Jerusalem and suffering, death, and resurrection (16:21—28:20). The object of the present discussion is to capture the full sweep of Matthew's portrait of the Son of God in Israel by tracing in bold strokes Matthew's sketch of him throughout 4:17—28:20.

Ministry in Israel and Repudiation

Having been declared by God to be his Son (3:17) and having proved himself to be perfectly obedient to God's will (4:1–11), Jesus takes up residence in Capernaum (4:12–16) and embarks upon his public ministry to Israel (4:17). The major summary passages 4:23; 9:35; and 11:1 indicate how Matthew conceives of this ministry: it is one of teaching, preaching, and healing.

Jesus commences his ministry by proclaiming, "Repent, for the kingdom of heaven is at hand!" (4:17). Next, he calls his first disciples (4:18–22), thus surrounding himself with eye- and ear-witnesses. Followed by the disciples and attracting huge crowds (4:23–25), he ascends a mountain and there programmatically teaches the will of God (5:1—7:29). Then, wandering in the area of Capernaum and traveling across the sea of Galilee and back, he performs ten mighty acts of deliverance, at the same time setting forth the nature and the cost of discipleship (8:1—9:34). At the height of his activity, he commissions the twelve to a ministry in Israel modeled on his own, one of preaching and healing though not of teaching (9:35—10:42).

The last of the three major summaries of Jesus' public ministry occurs at 11:1. In the section 11:2—16:20, which comprises the latter half of the second main part of Matthew's story, the tenor of the story changes. No longer does the motif of Jesus' teaching, preaching, and healing dominate the course of events. Instead, it is the motif of repudiation, which is coupled in turn with the motif of wonderment and speculation about the identity of Jesus. The two pericopes that call attention to these twin motifs are John the Baptist's question and Jesus' answer (11:2–6) and Jesus' rejection at Nazareth (13:53–58). These two pericopes stand out for two reasons: they are strategically located as far as the latter half of the second main part of Matthew's story is concerned (11:2—16:20); and each one contains both a question having to do with Jesus' identity (11:3; 13:55) and a prominent reference to "taking offense" at him (11:6; 13:57).

To trace the events of Matthew's story in the section 11:2—16:20, one should note that as a result of Jesus' widespread activity, his fame spreads throughout Palestine and even Syria.[44] Still, the spread of Jesus' fame and the thronging to him of the crowds are no indication that Israel has accepted him. Quite the contrary, Israel repudiates him (11:2—12:50),[45] and the gravest sign of this is that the Israelite leaders in the persons of the Pharisees take counsel on how to destroy him (12:14). Jesus' response to his repudiation is to declare Israel to be obdurate and to give public demonstration of this by addressing the crowds "in parables," that is, in speech they cannot understand (13:1–35). By contrast, he pronounces the disciples "blessed" (13:16–17) and explains to them the mysteries of the kingdom of heaven (13:11, 36–52).

Nor does Jesus fare any better in his home town of Nazareth. When the people hear him teach in the synagogue, they take offense at him (13:53–58). Even more ominously, news reaches Jesus that John the Baptist has been beheaded (14:1–12). This news prompts Jesus to embark on a series of journeys[46] that take him to deserted places, back and forth across the sea, and into gentile lands.[47]

It was said above that people in Israel also react to Jesus' public ministry in 11:2—16:20 by wondering or speculating about his identity. Thus, John the Baptist, expecting Jesus to execute final judgment (3:7–12), asks by way of the disciples he sends to him, "Are you the Coming One, or do we await another?" (11:2–3). The crowds, having witnessed a healing by Jesus, query one another, though in a manner that anticipates a negative reply, "This man cannot be the Son of David, can he?" (12:23). The hometown people of Nazareth, hearing Jesus teach in their synagogue, wonder in astonishment even as they take offense at him, "Is not this the carpenter's son?" (13:55). Herod Antipas, taking notice of the reports about Jesus, speculates, "This is John the Baptist; he has been raised from the dead, and therefore these miraculous powers are at work in him!" (14:2). And the disciples, having watched Jesus walk on the water, calm the wind, and rescue Peter from drowning, worship Jesus and affirm, "Truly you are the Son of God!" (14:33). In so doing, they in effect give answer to the earlier question they themselves had raised in an equally perilous situation at sea, "What sort of man is this, that even winds and sea obey him?" (8:27).[48]

All of these conflicting thoughts about Jesus Matthew combines into two contrasting positions that he juxtaposes in the climactic pericope of the second main part of his story, namely, the confession of Peter at Caesarea Philippi (16:13–20). To begin with, Jesus asks the disciples who the public imagines him to be, and they reply, "Some say John the Baptist, others say Elijah, and others Jeremiah or one of the prophets" (16:13–14). In other words, in the eyes of the Jewish public Jesus ranks as a prophet of some stature or another (cf. 21:11, 26, 46). This understanding of Jesus, however, is false: (a) Jesus cannot be John the Baptist, Elijah, Jeremiah, or one of the prophets because John, who is himself "Elijah," is the forerunner of Jesus (11:10, 14), and it is the task of Jeremiah and the prophets to "foretell" of Jesus;[49] and (b) the answer that Jesus is a prophet evokes no word of praise from Jesus (cf. 16:17).

In antithesis to his first question, Jesus next asks the disciples who they understand him to be, and Peter replies on behalf of all, "You are the Messiah, the Son of the living God!" (16:16). This answer of course is correct, as is manifest from the fact that it evokes a "blessing" from Jesus and is said by him to have been inspired by divine revelation (16:17). Accordingly, Matthew brings the second main part of his gospel-story, in which he describes Jesus' ministry to Israel and Israel's response to him, to its culmination by showing that whereas the public in Israel does not "receive"

Jesus and falsely conceives of him as being a prophet, the disciples confess him aright to be the Son of God.

Journey to Jerusalem and Suffering, Death, and Resurrection

Matthew devotes the third main part of his Gospel (16:21—28:20) to Jesus' journey to Jerusalem and to his suffering, death, and resurrection. To alert the reader to this, Matthew makes prominent use of three passion predictions (16:21; 17:22-23; 20:17-19).

Of interest is the way in which Matthew binds together the contents of this third part to form a coherent whole. While he does this primarily through the use of the passion predictions themselves, he also does it through the use of the literary device of the "journey." In 16:21 Jesus, uttering the first of his passion predictions, announces that he "goes" to Jerusalem. The effect of this announcement is to raise the activity of "going" to the level of a major motif within the third part of the Gospel. At first, Jesus continues to move within Galilee (16:21—18:35), but then he travels away from there into the regions of Judea beyond the Jordan (19:1—20:16), and at the last he journeys on to Jerusalem (20:17 28:15). After his resurrection, Jesus again returns to Galilee (28:16-20). Although the purpose of all such travel is not lost sight of thanks to the passion predictions, the travel itself must nevertheless be seen as a means in its own right by which Matthew unifies the materials of the third part of his Gospel.

To return briefly to Peter's confession of Jesus at Caesarea Philippi, Matthew has Jesus charge the disciples immediately following it to tell no one that he is the Messiah Son of God (16:16, 20). Why this prohibition? Because although the disciples showed that they knew who Jesus is, they were not as yet in any position to "make disciples of all nations," for they were still ignorant of the central purpose of his mission.

The central purpose of Jesus' mission is his suffering, and this is the first thing he tells the disciples in the section 16:21—28:20. Peter's response to Jesus' word is to reject out of hand the notion that he must suffer (16:22), and Jesus, in turn, reprimands Peter for this (16:23).

Nevertheless, six days later Jesus leads Peter, James, and John atop a high mountain. There he is suddenly transfigured before them, and from a cloud that overshadows them a voice exclaims, "This is my beloved Son, with whom I am well pleased; hear him!" (17:1-5). As at the baptism, the voice is that of God, and within the context of Matthew's Gospel it confirms the validity of Peter's recent confession (cf. 17:5 with 16:16). Equally important, however, is the fact that God does not simply repeat his baptismal proclamation but expands it, through the injunction to "hear him" (17:5). The stress, then, lies on this injunction, and necessarily so, for what the disciples must grasp in 16:21—28:20 is the truth of the very word of Jesus Peter has repudiated, namely, that about his passion (16:21-23). At what point the disciples will finally grasp this truth is made known in the command to silence Jesus gives the disciples: not until after he has been raised from the dead are the three to tell anyone about their experience atop the mountain (17:9).

Jesus and the three disciples descend from the mountain to those below, and all the disciples learn of the great power of faith (17:14-20). Then, the second passion prediction (17:22-23) and an exchange with Peter over the voluntary payment of the "half-shekel tax" (17:24-27) initiate Jesus' ecclesiological discourse to the disciples (18:1-35). His message is that loving concern for the neighbor and the spirit of forgiveness are to be the hallmarks of the community of believers in whose midst he, the Son of God, will ever be present.[50]

Leaving Galilee, Jesus now journeys more directly toward Jerusalem, traveling into the regions of Judea across the Jordan (19:1). Huge crowds again follow him, and he heals the sick (19:2). At the same time, he debates with his opponents (19:3-12) and the rich young man (19:16-22), instructs his disciples largely about ethical matters,[51] announces his impending passion a third time (20:17-19), and teaches the disciples that the essence of discipleship consists not in the enjoyment of privilege but in rendering service to others (20:20-28).

Outside Jericho, Jesus opens the eyes of two blind men who appeal to him as the "Son of David," that is, as the Messiah sent specifically to Israel (20:29-34). Next, surrounded by the crowds who hail him as the "Son of David," Jesus finally arrives at Jerusalem itself and enters the city with great ceremony (21:1-11). The tragedy, however, is that despite the fact that Jesus is called "Son of David," Israel remains blind to this truth: for the crowds, "Son of David" means no more than that Jesus is "the prophet . . . from Nazareth of Galilee" (21:11); and in the eyes of the leaders, Jesus could in no wise be the Son of David because he has already proved himself to be a false messiah who acts in collusion with the prince of demons (9:34; 12:24; cf. 27:63).

In Jerusalem, Jesus enters the temple and cleanses it, leaving that evening for Bethany (21:12–17). The next day, he returns to the temple, once again stressing on the way the power of prayer (21:18–22). In the temple, through his teaching of the people (21:23), his debates with the leaders,[52] his parables against Israel,[53] and his speech of woes against the scribes and Pharisees (chap. 23), he shows himself to be the Son of God who wields in the house of God the authority of God (21:23–27). When he leaves the temple, it is said to be "empty," which attests to the circumstance that God has chosen to replace it with his Son.[54]

One of the parables against Israel that Jesus narrates to the leaders while still in the temple is of particular importance to the development of Matthew's gospel-story: the parable of the wicked husbandmen (21:33–46). In it, Jesus sketches God's dealings with Israel in the history of salvation. He portrays God as the "owner of the vineyard" and himself as "the son" whom the owner calls "my son" and whom the wicked tenant-farmers kill (21:37–39). Quoting from scripture, Jesus likewise predicts that this "stone-son" whom the "builders" reject God will place "at the head of the corner," that is, vindicate through the miraculous act of the resurrection (21:42).

Noteworthy is the fact that by having the "owner of the vineyard" designate "the son" as "my son," Jesus adopts for himself the view of his identity which God had enunciated at both the baptism and the transfiguration (3:17; 17:5). Accordingly, Jesus is making himself out to be the Son of God, even while he is making the Israelite leaders out to be the murderous tenant-farmers. Because these identifications are by no means lost on the leaders and they reject them (21:45), they want to arrest Jesus (21:46). Ironically, however, in wanting to arrest Jesus, which is tantamount to denying the truth-claim of his parable, the leaders are unwittingly disavowing God's own understanding of Jesus' identity. Without doubt the leaders have grasped Jesus' parable intellectually, but they remain blind as to who he is for they will not, and cannot, accept his claim to be the Son of God.

From the temple, Jesus goes to the Mount of Olives, where he delivers to his disciples his eschatological discourse (chaps. 24—25). Although he foretells dire things to come, he also stresses that the task of his community of followers, despite dissension within and tribulation from without, is to preach the gospel of the kingdom throughout the world and to await in hope and watchfulness his sudden return in glory at the end of the age as the Judge of all.

With his passion at hand, Jesus Messiah, the Son of God, himself controls events that bring him to the cross (cf. 26:1–2).[55] On trial before the Sanhedrin (26:57–68), he again confronts the same Israelite leaders to whom he had narrated the parable of the wicked husbandmen (27:57, 59). As the presiding officer of the Sanhedrin, the high priest is privy to the claim to be the Son of God which Jesus had advanced in allegorical form in his parable. When, therefore, the high priest asks Jesus, ". . . are you the Messiah, the Son of God?" (26:63), he is at once reformulating Jesus' claim in nonallegorical terms and aiming to turn it against him in order to destroy him. Moreover, from his own standpoint the high priest succeeds, for Jesus' reply is affirmative ("[So] you have said"; 26:64; cf. 27:43). In consequence of Jesus' reply, the Sanhedrin, at the instigation of the high priest, condemns Jesus to death for blasphemy (26:65–66). And therein lies the irony of Jesus' fate: Jesus is made to die, but the only "crime" he has committed is that he has dared to claim to be the one God himself has twice said that he is, namely, the Messiah Son of God. Claiming to "see," the Israelite leaders show that they are "blind."

Bent on having Jesus put to death, the Israelite leaders deliver him to Pilate (chap. 27). At issue in the hearing before Pilate is whether Jesus is the "King of the Jews [Israel]."[56] Matthew has Jesus affirm that he is (27:11). In the ears of Pilate, this means that Jesus is an insurrectionist (27:37). But although Pilate does not believe for a moment that Jesus is in reality an insurrectionist, he nevertheless accedes to the Jewish demand that Jesus be crucified as such.[57] Wherein the truth of Jesus' kingship lies is in the fact that, as was observed above, he saves his people by suffering on their behalf (27:27–31, 42).

Placed on the cross, Jesus dies as the perfectly obedient and trusting Son of God (27:38–54). By his death, he brings to completion the mission for which he had been born and for which God had chosen and empowered him: he atones for sins, so that through him people have forgiveness (26:28), and thus he accomplishes salvation (1:21; 3:16–17). At the same time, his death also marks the destruction of the temple and the end of Israel's sacrificial cult (27:51). The confession of the Roman soldiers to the effect that he truly was the Son of God (27:54) serves at once to call attention to the circumstance that his earthly ministry is now at an end and to vindicate the claim to divine sonship he had raised at his trial. In the Matthean reference to both Jewish saints, who come forth from their tombs, and confessing Roman soldiers, one finds a prefigurement of the post-Easter church of people of Jewish and gentile origin (27:52–53, 54).

Matthew's concluding pericope (28:16–20) is the climax, not only of the third main part of his gospel-story (16:21—28:20), but also of his entire story. The Jesus who meets the eleven disciples atop the mountain in Galilee stands forth as the crucified but resurrected Son of God. Thus, he is the resurrected Son of God whose eschatological glory God revealed "proleptically" to Peter, James, and John on the mountain of the transfiguration (17:2, 5). Still, even as the resurrected Son of God, he remains the crucified Son of God ("the one who has been, and remains, the crucified"; 28:6; 27:54). Indeed, he is the rejected "stone-son" whom God has placed "at the head of the corner," that is, vindicated through resurrection and exalted to universal lordship (21:37, 42; 28:18). He is, in fact, Emmanuel, or "God with us," the Son conceived of the Spirit in whom God will abide with the disciples until the consummation of the age (1:20, 23; 28:20).

The disciples, in seeing Jesus Son of God as the resurrected one who bears the marks of the crucified one,[58] see him in new perspective. In the boat at sea and in the regions of Caesarea Philippi, the disciples confessed aright "who he is,"[59] but they did not as yet know of the central purpose of his mission, which was his passion. Atop the mountain of the transfiguration, God confirmed to Peter, James and John that the disciples' confession of Jesus was indeed valid, but he also enjoined them to "hear" Jesus (17:5); that is, he called upon them to pay heed to the very word of Jesus concerning his passion to which Peter had taken umbrage.[60] Here on the mountain in Galilee, it is the crucified, albeit also resurrected, Son of God who appears to the eleven (28:5–6, 16). Seeing Jesus as such, the disciples now comprehend, not only what they had earlier perceived as well, namely, that he is the Son of God, but also the central purpose of his mission, namely, his death on the cross and the salvation from sins he thereby accomplished. Still, this insight does not of itself guarantee that a post-Easter disciple is as a matter of course immune to the affliction of doubt, or little faith (28:17; cf. 14:28–33). Nonetheless, equipped with this insight, the disciples are not again commanded by Jesus, as previously, to silence concerning him (16:20; 17:9), but instead commissioned to go and make of all nations his disciples (28:19). In pursuit of this commission, the disciples move from Easter into the world Jesus described for them in his eschatological discourse of chapters 24—25.

Jesus as the Son of David

That Jesus Messiah is the Son of David is strongly affirmed by Matthew in his Gospel. Indeed, of the synoptic evangelists it is Matthew who develops the most expansive Son-of-David Christology.[61]

Just as strongly, however, Matthew also affirms that the divine sonship of Jesus transcends his Davidic sonship. This point Matthew makes both in chapter 1 and in the pericope on the question about David's son (22:41–46). In chapter 1, Matthew shows that whereas Jesus is the Son of David because Joseph son of David gives him his name and hence adopts him into his line,[62] he is the Son of God because he is miraculously conceived in Mary by a creative act of God's Holy Spirit (1:16, 18, 20).

In the pericope on the question about David's son (22:41–46), Matthew presents Jesus himself as arguing that, correct as it is to look upon the Messiah as being the Son of David, it is at the same time insufficient. In debate with the Pharisees, Jesus confounds them a problem of antinomy. The question he puts to them is: How is it possible for the Messiah to be both the "son" of David and the "lord" of David when these two views are ostensibly contradictory? Although Jesus leaves the answer to be inferred, the reader of the Gospel can well supply it: the Messiah is the "son" of David because he stands in the line of David (1:1, 6, 25); at the same time, the Messiah is also the "lord" of David because he is the Son of God and therefore of higher station and authority than David (3:16–17; 17:5).

But although Matthew is quick to affirm that the Davidic sonship of Jesus is transcended by his divine sonship, the titles Son of God and Son of David are not to be viewed as antithetic to each other. For Matthew, Jesus Son of God is the royal Messiah from the line of David.

What use does Matthew make of the title "Son of David" in his Gospel? In this connection, two things stand out. The first is that Matthew sharply restricts the scope of this title. And the second is that he employs it both positively, to assert that Jesus does in fact stand in the line of David and fulfill messianic expectation associated with his house, and polemically, to underline the guilt that devolves upon Israel for not receiving the one in whom it especially was to find blessing and salvation.

That Matthew sharply restricts the scope of the title Son of David is plain to see. To begin with, "Son of David" is applied only to the earthly Jesus and not to the crucified and exalted Jesus. Second, the disciples do not relate to Jesus on the basis of this title, for never do they confess or even address him as the Son of David. Third, apart from Jesus' entry into Jerusalem, this title is associated exclusively with the activity of "healing." Never, for example, is Jesus described as "teaching" or "preaching" as the Son of David. And fourth, even in regard to the activity of healing, except for the "blind and lame" in the temple (21:14), it is only individuals and never large numbers of people who are made well by the Son of David.

Both the positive and the polemical tone of the title Son of David is likewise readily apparent. The persons Jesus heals as Son of David are, respectively, two "blind men" (9:27–31), a "blind and dumb man" (12:22), the "daughter" of a gentile woman (15:21–28), another two "blind men" (20:29–34), and the "blind and lame" in the temple (21:14). These persons are "no-accounts" in Israel, as are the "children" who hail Jesus as the Son of David in the temple (21:15) and the Canaanite "woman" who pleads the case of her daughter (15:21–22). These "no-accounts" are able to "see" and "confess" what Israel will not, namely, that Jesus is its Messiah. As such, their example underlines the guilt that is Israel's for its repudiation of Jesus.

That there is in truth no recognition on Israel's part of Jesus as the Son of David is made abundantly clear by Matthew. The Israelite leaders witness the healing activity of the Son of David, but this only provokes them to indignation (21:15) or motivates them to charge Jesus with being an emissary of Satan (9:32–34; 12:22–24). The crowds at least pose the question of whether he is the Son of David, but the manner in which they frame it anticipates, in the Greek original, a negative reply: "This can't be the Son of David, can it?" (12:23). When Jesus enters Jerusalem and the crowds do hail him as the Son of David, they explain that this title means no more to them than that he is "the prophet . . . from Nazareth" (21:9–11).

On balance, then, Matthew's use of the title Son of David suggests that two tendencies are at work to guide this use. On the one hand, Matthew shows that he is surely concerned to present Jesus as the Son of David, the royal Messiah sent to save Israel whom Joseph son of David adopts into his line. On the other hand, Matthew is also at pains to show that however important the Davidic sonship of Jesus may be, it is transcended by his divine sonship.

Jesus as Lord

Some Matthean scholars maintain, on largely unexamined grounds, that "Lord," or "Kyrios" *(kyrios)*, is the chief christological title with which Matthew operates.[63] The evidence, however, suggests that it is not nearly so imposing as this.

Apart from the parables, Matthew uses the term *kyrios* on at least three levels. For instance, at 27:63 purely conventional usage dictates that the Israelite leaders address Pilate with the equivalent of the English "sir." Numerous times it is a designation for "God."[64] And of course it also occurs as a designation for Jesus.

Used of Jesus, *kyrios* is a christological title in the First Gospel only in a qualified sense.[65] It is not of the same nature as are such terms as "Messiah," "King of the Jews," "Son of Abraham," "Son of David," and "Son of God." The purpose of these is to tell the reader "who Jesus is" and to ascribe to him a particular status and function. By way of illustration, take "Son of Abraham," "Son of David," and "Son of God." "Son of Abraham" describes Jesus as the supreme heir of Abraham in whom the entire history of Israel reaches its culmination and the gentiles find blessing (1:17; 8:11). Similarly, "Son of David" describes Jesus as the long-promised scion of David in whom Israel especially is to find blessing (1:6; 21:5, 9). And "Son of God," while it points to Jesus as the royal Messiah from the line of David and of Abraham, nevertheless lays stress on the unique filial relationship that Jesus has with God, his Father, and the implications this holds for the salvation of humankind.[66]

By contrast, *kyrios* is a relational term. Except for Jesus himself, it crosses the lips primarily of the disciples or those who come to Jesus trusting that he can heal or save (cf. 8:21, 28). In using it, persons predicate to Jesus (or he to himself) an exalted station and divine authority. Moreover, such station and authority can be his, for example, as Messiah,[67] Son of David ("Have mercy on me Lord, Son of David"; 15:22),[68] Son of God,[69] or in his role as end-time Judge.[70] In other words, *kyrios* is a christological title of a peculiar sort because it functions not to confer on Jesus an "office" as such but to ascribe exalted station and divine authority to him in his capacity as Messiah, Son of David, Son of God, or end-time Judge.

Jesus as the Son of Man

If the titular status of *kyrios* in Matthew's Gospel is not unambiguous, the same is true of "the Son of man."[71] In fact, whether it is better to regard "the Son of man" more maximally as a christological title or more minimally as a technical term is not easy to say.

In favor of the view that "the Son of man" is a title are at least three factors. For one thing, the use to which it is put is such that, overall, it reflects the peculiar contours of the ministry of Jesus: Jesus designates himself as "the Son of man" in association with his earthly activity,[72] with his suffering, death, and resurrection,[73] and with his anticipated parousia.[74] The upshot is that "the Son of man" is a term that applies to Jesus in a way in which it cannot be applied to any other human being. For another thing, "the Son of man" is also unique because it occurs solely in Jesus' mouth, is always definite in form ("the" Son of man), and always refers to him exclusively. And third, Jesus fulfills OT prophecy as the one who calls himself "the Son of man,"[75] which is further indication that this term possesses a distinctiveness that is comparable to that of the other major titles.

But weighty though these three factors are, opposite them stands a fourth factor that suggests just as strongly that "the Son of man" ought not be construed as a title but merely as a technical term: unlike the other major titles, "the Son of man" seems not to be employed in Matthew's gospel-story to set forth the identity of Jesus (i.e., to make known "who he is"). Four examples illustrate this well. First, unlike such titles as "Messiah," "King of the Jews [Israel]," "Son of David," and "Son of God," no character in Matthew's story, neither transcendent being nor human being, ever says or asks of Jesus, "This is (You are; Are you? Is this?) the Son of man."[76] Since these other titles are "confessional" in nature and have as their purpose to specify who Jesus is, the obvious inference to be drawn from this phenomenon is that "the Son of man" is different in nature from them and does not have as its purpose to specify who he is.

Another indication that "the Son of man" does not function to explicate "who Jesus is" is the fact that although Jesus frequently employs it in public to refer to himself, the thought occurs neither to the Jews nor to the disciples to identify him as such. Consider the Jews. In the full hearing of the crowd(s)[77] and of the Jewish leaders,[78] Jesus designates himself as "the Son of man." Yet, when the question of Jesus' identity arises, the Jewish leaders and public think of him as being, not "the Son of man," but either as "that deceiver" who is in collusion with the prince of demons[79] or as a "prophet,"[80] namely, John the Baptist, Elijah, Jeremiah, or one of the prophets (16:14; also 14:2).

Or take the disciples. In their hearing, too, Jesus repeatedly calls himself "the Son of man."[81] But this notwithstanding, when the disciples confess Jesus in the boat on the sea or when Jesus puts to them the question of his identity in the regions of Caesarea Philippi, the affirmation they make is not that he is "the Son of man" but the "Son of God" (14:33; 16:15-16).

In the third place, the two key passages 16:13 and 26:63 reveal in especially telling fashion that "the Son of man" does not serve in Matthew's Gospel to set forth the identity of Jesus. At 16:13, Jesus asks the disciples, "Who do men say that the Son of man is?" If the disciples' reply to Jesus is not to be absurd ("Men say that the Son of man is the Son of man"), Jesus' very question excludes the possibility that "the Son of man" discloses his identity. And what of the words of the high priest in 26:63? Although Jesus has, as was noted above, referred to himself in public and on more than one occasion during his ministry as "the Son of man," the high priest, inquiring after his true identity, does not place him under oath at his trial to declare before the Sanhedrin whether he is "the Son of man" but whether he is the "Messiah, the Son of God."

And last, that the function of "the Son of man" is not to make known "who Jesus is" is also to be inferred from the fact that this term is conspicuously absent from the first main part of Matthew's story (1:1—4:16). The aim of this part is to present Jesus to the reader so that the reader will, throughout the rest of the story, know "who Jesus is." This explains why the major designations by means of which Matthew identifies Jesus all stand out prominently in this part: "Jesus," "Jesus Christ," "Messiah," "Son of David," "King of the Jews," and "Son of God." By contrast, Matthew does not introduce the expression "the Son of man" into his story until as late as 8:20. Moreover, when he does introduce it, he does so unobtrusively, for the reader does not anticipate its sudden use, and the focus of the text is neither on the expression itself nor on the topic of Jesus' identity but on the theme of discipleship. Literarily, it is difficult to see from the way Matthew first acquaints the reader with "the Son of man" that it is intended to inform the reader of "who Jesus is."

In the final analysis, then, is "the Son of man" in Matthew's Gospel a christological title or is it merely a technical term? The answer is that as long as one keeps in mind the fact that "the Son of man," like the other major titles, refers exclusively to Jesus but that, unlike them, it does not set forth his identity, one is free, it would seem, to place the stress on either side of the equation and hence to view "the Son of man" as either. But regardless of whether one decides to view "the Son of man" as title or technical term, crucial to gaining a right understanding of it is to know what it means, how it properly functions in the gospel-story, and what impact Matthew's use of it has upon this story. In the interest of answering these questions, "the Son of man" may be defined as the designation by means of which Jesus points to himself as "the (this) man" in public or in view of the public (or "world") as he discharges his ministry to Israel or speaks of his passion or of his parousia.

Technically, the translation of the Greek original of "the Son of man" is "the man," or "the human being." Still, correct as this translation is, one cannot simply substitute "the man" or "the human being" each time "the Son of man" occurs in Matthew's Gospel without incurring a problem. The problem one incurs is that although "the Son of man" refers without exception to Jesus alone, the translation "the man," or "the human being," does not always make it as immediately obvious as it must be that Jesus is in fact the one being spoken of. Cases in point are such passages as 8:20 ("Foxes have holes and birds of the air nests, but 'the man' has nowhere to lay his head") and 12:32 ("And whoever says a word against 'the man' will be forgiven . . ."). To circumvent this problem, it is preferable to render in English the Greek original of "the Son of man" with the expression "this man." "This man" is what may be termed a translational equivalent: it captures in English the force of the Greek original of "the Son of man."[82] Substitution of "this man" for "the Son of man" each time the latter occurs makes it unmistakably clear that "the man" being referred to is in each instance Jesus ("Foxes have holes and birds of the air nests, but 'this man' has nowhere to lay his head"; "And whoever says a word against 'this man' will be forgiven . . .").

If "the man" is an accurate translation of the underlying Greek of "the Son of man" and "this man" is its translational equivalent, it becomes eminently clear how Jesus can, as was noted above, openly speak of himself as the Son of man in Matthew's gospel-story without at the same time ever having any character give even the slightest indication that he or she thinks that Jesus is thereby divulging his identity. If "the Son of man" has the force of "this man," then it can occur in Jesus' mouth frequently and in public and yet never occasion the disclosure of his identity. Still, precisely because Jesus' use of "the Son of man" does not disclose his identity, the question necessarily arises: What specifically is the identity of Jesus the Son of man? On this score, Matthew is unambiguous, pointing the reader to the words Peter utters at Caesarea Philippi. Who, then, is Jesus the Son of man—i.e., Who is "this man" Jesus? (16:13)? He is the Son of God (16:16). And lest one object that this answer is but the words of Peter, one will recall that Peter's answer tallies with the declarations God himself makes both following the baptism and at the transfiguration (3:17; 17:5). Then, too, for one to recognize that the Son of man in Matthew's Gospel is to be identified as the Son of God is also of benefit for gaining insight into yet another problem area. In the passages 16:27 and 25:34, the expressions "his Father" and "my Father" occur with reference to Jesus as the Son of man. Seen properly, these expressions likewise attest to the identity of Jesus the Son of man: Jesus the Son of man ("this man" Jesus), in referring to God as "my Father," tacitly bears witness that he is the Son of God.

Should the expression "this man" capture in English the meaning of the Greek that lies behind "the Son of man," how does the latter function in Matthew's Gospel? It does not function "confessionally," as has been pointed out, but as a "public designation." In what sense is it a "public designation"?

"The Son of man" is a "public designation" in the sense that it is primarily with an eye to the "world," Jews and Gentiles and especially opponents, that Jesus calls himself the Son of man. To verify this, consider the following. In the earthly Son-of-man sayings, it is in view of the Jewish public (16:13) or of the world (13:36–37) or in the audience of the crowds,[83] of some of the scribes,[84] and of the Pharisees[85] that Jesus refers to himself as the Son of man. In the suffering Son-of-man sayings, it is to some of the scribes and Pharisees (12:38, 40) or to the disciples but in view of Judas,[86] of "men"[87] and "sinners" (26:45), of the Jewish leaders (20:18), of gentiles (20:19) and of the rulers of the gentiles (20:25, 28) that Jesus speaks of himself as the Son of man. And in the future Son-of-man sayings, it is in view of all the nations (Israel, the gentiles, the Jewish leaders, but also the disciples [since they, too, must at the Latter Day undergo judgment])[88] that Jesus terms himself the Son of man. In short, it is this orientation toward the "world" in Jesus' use of "the Son of man" that marks this designation as "public" in nature.

A final question remains to be discussed: What impact does Matthew's use of "the Son of man" have upon his gospel-story? To answer this question, it is helpful to compare the overall role "the Son of man" plays with that family of titles the most important of which is "Son of God" (e.g., "Messiah," "King of the Jews [Israel]" and "Son of David"). Briefly put, "Son of God" is a "confessional title" the purpose of which is to identify Jesus.[89] By contrast, "the Son of man" is a "public designation": it is not used by Jesus to divulge his identity but to refer to himself as "the man," or "the human being" ("this man," or "this human being"). The purpose for which Jesus employs this designation is multiple: to assert his divine authority in the face of public opposition; to tell his disciples that the "public," or "world" (Jews and gentiles), will cause him to suffer and put him to death; and to predict that he whom the world puts to death God will vindicate, first, through the resurrection, and later, by means of his return as Judge of all. Consequently, through Jesus' use of the public designation of the Son of man, Matthew calls attention to the twin elements of "conflict" and "vindication." In Matthew's purview, these mark the interaction of Jesus with the public, or world, that does not receive him as the one he is, namely, the Son of God.

CHAPTER THREE

MATTHEW'S UNDERSTANDING OF THE KINGDOM OF HEAVEN

The single most comprehensive concept in the First Gospel is the "kingdom of heaven (God)." It denotes, as was observed in chapter 1, that "God rules (reigns)." The expression the "rule (reign) of God" is an accurate paraphrase of it.

In setting forth his portrait of Jesus, Matthew makes effective use, as was seen in the last chapter, of the chief structural feature of his Gospel, his topical outline: Matthew first presents Jesus to the reader (1:1—4:16), and then tells of his ministry to Israel and repudiation (4:17—16:20) and of his journey to Jerusalem and suffering, death, and resurrection (16:21—28:20). By the same token, Matthew employs the second chief structural feature of his Gospel, his view of the history of salvation, to advance his concept of the kingdom of heaven.

Concerning Matthew's view of the history of salvation, he distinguishes, it will be recalled, between the "time of Israel (OT)" as the time of prophecy and the "time of Jesus (earthly—exalted)" as the time of fulfillment. Moreover, he also divides the broad time of Jesus, extending from birth to parousia, into discernible segments: the ministries to Israel of John, of the earthly Jesus, and of the disciples, and the ministry to the world of the post-Easter church. Now John, Jesus, and the disciples all proclaim that the "kingdom of heaven is at hand,"[1] and both Jesus and the church following Easter proclaim the "gospel of the kingdom."[2] The focal point of all such "kingdom proclamation" is, of course, the activity of God in Jesus Messiah, his Son. In terms of the central thought controlling the First Gospel, such divine activity is to be understood as God's drawing near with his eschatological rule in the person of his Son Jesus to dwell to the end of the age with his people, the church (1:23; 18:20; 28:20).

The goal of the present chapter is to examine various aspects of the eschatological rule of God, or the kingdom of heaven, as Matthew describes it. In pursuit of this goal, one thing to be kept in mind is the essentially christological orientation of this theological concept: Matthew insists that it is in Jesus Messiah, the Son of God, that one encounters the kingdom of heaven.

The Kingdom of Heaven

Although the expression "the kingdom of heaven" does not occur as a fixed phrase in the OT, conceptually its roots are embedded there. The idea that "God rules," that he is "King," is one of Israel's elemental affirmations.[3]

According to first-century Jewish thought, God's kingly rule is eternal and encompasses the entire world and all of the nations and powers in it. In the present age, however, God's sovereignty is fully acknowledged only in Israel. Still, the day is rapidly approaching when God will suddenly break into history, openly manifest himself in splendor as the Ruler of all, and in so doing free his people from heathen bondage and subject all nations to his holy will.

To turn to the First Gospel, the immediate task is to discuss the "salvation-historical," the "cosmic," and the "ethical" dimensions of Matthew's concept of the kingdom of heaven.

The Salvation-Historical Dimension of the Kingdom

The salvation-historical dimension of the kingdom of heaven refers to the fact that, for Matthew, the kingdom is a transcendent, eschatological reality that confronts people already in the present but will be consummated only in the future. Thus, Matthew pictures, as noted last chapter, John, Jesus, and the disciples as proclaiming in Israel that the "kingdom of heaven is at hand" (*ēggiken*) (3:2; 4:17; 10:7). The verb *ēggiken* denotes a "coming near," an "approaching," that is spatial or temporal in character. "Spatially," the kingdom has drawn near because God in the person of his Son even now resides with those who live in the sphere of his rule (1:23; 18:20; 28:20). Under the aegis of the earthly and exalted Son of God, the will of the Father who is in heaven above is not hidden but known on earth, and the disciples of Jesus respond to it with lives that reflect the greater righteousness.[4]

"Temporally," too, the kingdom of heaven has drawn near. Although the kingdom, to Matthew's way of thinking, belongs to the future, in the person of Jesus Son of God it has come upon the present so as radically to qualify it.[5] Consequently, the present is to be viewed in the light of the future and everything seen as moving toward the consummation and Jesus' parousia.[6]

The "spatial" and the "temporal" aspects of the drawing near of the kingdom of heaven are part and parcel of its "eschatological" nature. Associated with this adjective are notions about both the time and the ultimate significance of the kingdom. Matthew, for example, holds the kingdom of heaven to be an eschatological reality because the proclamation of its nearness occurs in the "time of Jesus (earthly—exalted)," the "last times" that precede the consummation and are inaugurated by the conception and birth of Jesus Messiah (1:23).

But the kingdom is also an eschatological reality in Matthew's perspective because the proclamation of its nearness is of ultimate significance for both Israel and the gentiles. The tenor of this proclamation is, after all, that God with his rule has in fact drawn near to humankind in his Son. In such proclamation, Israel and the nations encounter the rule of God, a rule that, again, is tending toward its consummation. God's will is that the proclamation of his kingdom be received with repentance and faith, and that people enter the sphere of his sovereignty to their salvation. They can, however, reject the word and at the last perish.

From the discussion thus far, it should already be clear that the kingdom of heaven is a reality that can only be described in terms of both the present and the future. Indeed, the verb *ēggiken*, mentioned above, harbors within it this very tension between present and future. On the one hand, it connotes that the kingdom is indeed near, so near that in the person of the earthly and exalted Son of God the authority (power) of God impinges upon the present and decisively qualifies it. On the other hand, it connotes that the kingdom has not yet arrived, for God has not yet miraculously consummated his rule in all power and outward splendor. When will this take place? As the apocalyptic Son-of-man sayings stipulate, this will take place at the end of the age when the exalted Jesus returns for judgment.

If the verb *ēggiken* at 3:2; 4:17; and 10:7 embodies a tension between the present and the future modes of the kingdom, in numerous places in the Gospel the stress is more clearly on either the one pole or the other. For example, in a wide variety of ways Matthew expresses the conviction that in the recent past God has been, and is presently, at work in his Son to visit people with his rule. One way Matthew expresses this conviction is through the use of the schema of prophecy and fulfillment, especially as the latter is applied in the case of the formula quotations. Another way is by attributing to Jesus divine authority, so that he delivers the Sermon on the Mount as the Son who stands above Moses (chaps. 5—7) and also dares to forgive sins (9:2, 5–6), incurring thereby the charge of blasphemy (9:3).

Yet a third way in which Matthew points to the presence of the kingdom in Jesus is through his appropriation from the tradition of a number of eschatological images. Pertinent are the following. The Matthean Jesus declares that "something greater" than either Jonah or Solomon is here (12:41–42). He warns that one should not attempt to place a "piece of unshrunk cloth" on an old garment (9:16) or to put "new wine" in old wineskins (9:17). He designates himself in quotation of the OT as the "shepherd" (26:31) and describes his mission in terms of gathering the flock.[7] He refers to himself also as the "bridegroom" (9:15) and to his time as one of joy and celebration as at a wedding.[8] And he anticipates the eschatological banquet[9] by granting table fellowship to toll collectors and sinners (cf. 9:10; 11:19).

In his use of eschatological imagery, one word for which Matthew shows great affinity is *makarios* ("blessed"). This word, which portrays the present in the light of the future, bears strong witness to the kingdom as a present reality in that it attests to the unique religious joy that springs from those who share in the salvation God bestows upon all who live in the sphere of his sovereignty. These people are "blessed," for they have not taken offense at Jesus Messiah (cf. 11:6) but have received in faith the revelation imparted by his Father to the effect that he is the Son of God (cf. 16:17). Because of this, they can be said to have eyes that see and ears that hear the many things the prophets and righteous ones desired to see and hear but were not privileged to do so (13:16–17). In point of fact, these people are like faithful slaves who do the will of their lord,[10] who reflect in their lives the eschatological reversal of values,[11] and who rejoice in the face of persecution, knowing that their reward lies with God and that in enduring affliction they are following in the footsteps of the OT prophets (cf. 5:10–12).

In the fourth place, there are three passages in the First Gospel which merit special attention because they depict the kingdom in especially striking fashion as a present reality. The one passage is 12:28. In substance, it underlines an important truth not yet mentioned, namely, that the rule of

God effects the destruction of the rule of Satan. Of equal interest, however, is the circumstance that Matthew does not hesitate in this verse to make the kingdom the subject of a verb in the past (aorist) tense: "The kingdom of God 'has come' *(ephthasen)* upon you." In the whole of the Gospel, this passage represents one of Matthew's most direct overtures to "realized" eschatology.

The second passage is 21:43. Here "the kingdom of God" functions as the subject of a double predicate. As a saying of the earthly Jesus, the two verbs have been cast in the future tense. But the thing to note is that, from Matthew's vantage point in history, these verbs refer to an event of the immediate past. At any rate, this saying ascribes to the kingdom such a degree of reality in the present that it can "be taken away" *(arthēsetai)* by God from Israel and "be given" *(dothēsetai)* to another nation that will produce its fruits.

The third passage is 11:12. As before, the kingdom is the subject of the sentence, but this time the verb is in the present tense *(biazetai)*. As to its meaning, 11:12 is difficult to interpret, but the following translation seems to capture its intention: "From the days of John the Baptist until now the kingdom of heaven has suffered violence, and violent ones plunder it." Who, specifically, are these "violent ones"? From Matthew's standpoint, they are the devil and all the false Christians, Israelites, and gentiles who are his "sons" ("the sons of the Evil One"), those who resist the rule of God and "plunder" it in that through various means they lead "sons of the kingdom" astray and bring them to fall.[12] Be that as it may, what is noteworthy about 11:12 is that it describes the kingdom as a sphere that is present among people in such measure that it can be said to be vulnerable to attack from the side of its enemies.

Last, also in the time following Easter and leading up to the parousia Matthew portrays the kingdom as a present reality (13:36–39). In this time, which is Matthew's own time of the church, the risen and exalted Jesus is seen as ruling over the world (13:38; cf. 28:18). Moreover, what he does in the world is to raise up "sons of the kingdom" (13:38). How does he do this? Through the worldwide missionary efforts of his church as he leads people to become his disciples and so to join the ranks of those who confess him to be the Son of God and who live in the sphere of God's eschatological rule.[13]

If Matthew emphasizes the fact that God is presently at work in his Son Jesus to bring his eschatological kingdom to people, he sketches with even greater vividness the future consummation of the kingdom. As Matthew envisages it, the event that inaugurates the future kingdom will unfold in the following sequence: the forces of nature will suddenly fall into disarray; the exalted Jesus will be seen coming on the clouds of heaven in power and great glory; all the nations will be gathered before him; he will separate them into two groups; and he will pronounce judgment on them, thus determining who will "inherit the kingdom" that has been prepared from the foundation of the world and who will "go away into eternal punishment."[14]

Matthew is at pains in painting his portrait of the future kingdom to show that it is continuous with God's kingly activity in the present. The parables of the tares, mustard seed, leaven, and net illustrate this well. Thus, although the major point of the parable of the tares (13:24–30) is that darnel and wheat are to be allowed to grow side by side until the harvest (13:30a), it is nonetheless from the sowing of the seed by the farmer (the ministry of the earthly Jesus) that the harvest (the consummation of the age and the inauguration of the future kingdom by the exalted Jesus) finally results. The twin parables of the mustard seed (13:31–32) and of the leaven (13:33) put it this way: from something most insignificant, like a mustard seed or a little lump of leaven placed in dough (the ministry of Jesus), there issues something most magnificent, like the mustard "tree" or the great mass of fully leavened bread (the future kingdom). The parable of the net (13:47–50) advances this truth as follows: the gathering of the fish (the growth of the church in this age owing to its missionary proclamation of the kingdom) is necessarily followed by the separation of the fish (the church, too, will undergo judgment at the consummation).

As far as Jesus himself and the righteous are concerned, Matthew shows that the future kingdom means, respectively, vindication and the perfect realization of hope. With respect to Jesus, the irony is that he who suffers crucifixion at the hands of Jew and gentile and is utterly rejected is the very one whom God has chosen to return at the consummation as the Judge and Ruler of all.[15] To Jesus as well the saying applies: "For there is nothing hidden which shall not be revealed . . ." (10:26).

For the righteous, Matthew brings into play a wide variety of word-pictures in order to characterize the future kingdom as the perfect realization of hope. Matthew depicts the future kingdom, for example, as a realm the righteous will "enter,"[16] "go into" (21:31), or "inherit" (25:34), and what these idioms signify is evident from parallel passages that tell of "entering life,"[17] "entering the joy of your Lord,"[18] or "inheriting eternal life" (19:29). Of course the contrary is equally true: one can "not enter,"[19] be shut out (25:10), or be "thrown out,"[20] and therefore excluded from the latter-day kingdom. In addition, the bliss the righteous will experience in the future kingdom is described in figurative language that refers to Jesus as the eschatological "bridegroom,"[21] to the consummated kingdom as a "wedding celebration" (25:10) or as a banquet,[22] and to the righteous as perfected ones who "shine as the sun" (13:43). And the reception of the "reward" that the future kingdom connotes for the righteous comes to expression in all those sayings that dwell on the reversal of their condition: he who loses his life will find it (10:39); the last will be first;[23] he who humbles himself will be exalted (23:12); and the radical changes enumerated by the Beatitudes (cf. 5:3–10).

The overall purpose of this discussion has been to set forth the salvation-historical dimension of Matthew's concept of the kingdom of heaven. This dimension dominates the concept, and one facet of it still to be covered more thoroughly is the crisis that the nearness of the kingdom precipitates for persons, whether Israelite or gentile. Nevertheless, what is clear from the preceding is that Matthew regards the kingdom of heaven as an exclusively eschatological reality: it is openly proclaimed by John, the earthly Jesus, the disciples, and the church in the "time of Jesus (earthly—exalted)" (the "last times"), and such proclamation of the kingdom is of ultimate significance for Israel and for the nations. In other respects, the kingdom is a reality that is at once present and future: from the unprecedented activity of God in the person of Jesus in the present there will issue in the future the consummated kingdom of heaven. Christologically, the kingdom draws near in the present in the person of Jesus Messiah, the Son of God, and those who accept the gospel of the kingdom join the community of his disciples and experience the rule of God under his aegis. At the same time, these disciples also know that in post-Easter times this same Jesus, now as the risen and exalted One, works through his ambassadors to lead people in the world to know and confess him to be the Son of God. Then, too, at the end of time he, the Judge and Ruler of all, will return and inaugurate the future, splendid kingdom to the salvation of the righteous and the damnation of the wicked. Accordingly, the arrival of the future kingdom means the "public" vindication of Jesus, the one crucified and rejected, and, for the righteous, the perfect realization of their hope.

The Cosmic Dimension of the Kingdom

The cosmic dimension of Matthew's concept of the kingdom of heaven has to do with the oft-maligned notion of the "growth" of the kingdom. On this score, however, it should go without saying that the old liberal idea that the kingdom is to be regarded as a social, moral, or spiritual force that will gradually spread throughout the world as it captures the hearts of people, is foreign to the mind of Matthew. Moreover, from one standpoint Matthew, too, would reject any suggestion that the kingdom could be said to grow: he, like his Jewish contemporaries and Israelite predecessors, believes that God is, and always has been, the "Lord of heaven and earth."[24]

The thought that the kingdom grows relates to Matthew's understanding of the course of the kingdom in the world as a present reality that confronts people in the "time of Jesus." As Matthew sees it, God in heaven reigns indeed over all things, but he has determined in the last times to draw near to humankind in the person of Jesus Messiah, his Son. Still, the nearness of God in the person of his Son and, by extension, in the church's post-Easter proclamation of the gospel of the kingdom, is not something unambiguous. On the contrary, it is something that can be perceived only by means of divine revelation.[25] Nevertheless, as the church in post-Easter times proclaims the gospel of the kingdom to the nations,[26] persons will in truth be led to acknowledge the rule of God in Jesus, his Son, and, as they become disciples of Jesus, the kingdom can in fact be described as growing. Finally, at the consummation of the age, God in the person of the exalted Jesus will wondrously establish his rule in glory over all the "tribes of the earth" (24:30). Accordingly, the course of the kingdom in the world during the "time of Jesus" is that from the "small beginnings" of Jesus Messiah, the Son of God, and his initial disciples,[27] the kingdom, through the agency of the post-Easter church,[28] "grows" as the gospel is proclaimed to the nations, and, at the last, when the exalted Jesus shall burst into history, this kingdom will visibly be established over all.

Several parabolic units in the Gospel document this view of the growth of the kingdom particularly well. In the parable of the mustard seed (13:31–32), for instance, the "mustard seed," which was proverbial among the Jews as the most minute of quantities, is depicted as "growing" until, miraculously, it becomes a "tree" in which the birds from heaven nest, an image which in the OT stands for a mighty empire.[29] In the parable of the leaven (13:33), the image is that of the little lump of "yeast" causing the dough to swell until the "whole" mass has become fully leavened. In the parable of the net (13:47–50), the "drag-net" is described as "gathering in" fish of every kind until that time comes when the good fish must be separated from the bad. In the interpretation of the parable of the tares (13:36–43), the text identifies the "field" over which the exalted Jesus at the consummation will suddenly be revealed as ruling with the entire "world" *(kosmos)*. And in the so-called parable of the last judgment (25:31–46), the exalted Jesus is portrayed as seated on the throne of his glory with all the nations of the earth standing before him in acknowledgment of his universal rule. As was stated above, from small, seemingly insignificant, beginnings Matthew pictures the kingdom as ultimately and miraculously cosmic in scope.

The Ethical Dimension of the Kingdom

By the ethical, or personal, dimension of Matthew's concept of the kingdom of heaven is meant the new life that can result from a person's encounter with the reign of God. Of course the occasion for such encounter is the presence of the kingdom in Jesus Messiah, the earthly and exalted Son of God, and therefore in the proclamation by him and his church of "the gospel of the kingdom."

In a number of passages, Matthew makes it clear that encounter with the earthly Jesus placed a person in a crisis of decision.[30] As for Matthew's own time of the church following Easter, encounter with the gospel of the kingdom precipitates the same crisis.[31] In confrontation with the words and deeds of the earthly Jesus, a person faced the choice of "repenting" and "entering" the gracious sphere of the kingdom[32] or of rejecting Jesus as the Messiah (cf. chaps. 11–12). In confrontation with the church's proclamation of the gospel of the kingdom, one either "understands" the word (cf. 13:23) and is "baptized" (cf. 28:19) and observes all that Jesus has commanded,[33] or one does "not understand" the word and hence falls under the power of Satan (cf. 13:19, 38c–39a). Whoever understands the gospel of the kingdom may be compared to a "good tree" that produces "good fruit"[34] or to a "good man" who brings forth "good things" out of his "good treasure" (12:35), that is to say, this person, like Jesus Son of God himself (cf. 26:42), "does the will of the heavenly Father."[35] Such a person abounds in righteousness more than the scribes and Pharisees

(5:20) and will, at the coming of the exalted Jesus, be identified by him as one of the "righteous"[36] who will "inherit eternal life" (25:46) and "shine [in perfection] as the sun in the kingdom of their Father" (13:43).

On the other hand, those who have fallen under the power of Satan are "evil ones,"[37] who may be compared to a "bad tree" that produces "bad fruit,"[38] or to an "evil man" who brings forth "evil things" from his "evil treasure" (12:35). At the latter day, the exalted Jesus will designate these people as the "accursed" (25:41), and they will be cast into the "fiery furnace"[39] or into the "outer darkness" (8:12) where they will experience "eternal punishment" (25:46), such as the "weeping and gnashing of teeth."[40] So again, encounter with the kingdom means that a person must decide: will he or she enter the "narrow gate" and take the "hard way" that leads to "life," or will he or she enter the "wide gate" and take the "broad way" that leads to "destruction" (7:13-14)?

This delineation of Matthew's understanding of the ethical, or personal, dimension of the kingdom brings to a close the long discussion of Matthew's broad concept of the kingdom of heaven. Our concern now is to discuss the kingdom as it relates, respectively, to the kingdom of Satan, to Israel and to the nations, and, next chapter, to the church.

The Kingdom of Heaven and the Kingdom of Satan

Matthew's concept of the kingdom of heaven involves a pronounced dualism that depicts Jesus and Satan as engaged in mortal struggle until the time of the consummation itself. The following is a sketch of this struggle.

Matthew's portrait of the arch-adversary of Jesus is that of a transcendent being who stands in unmitigated opposition to the kingdom of heaven.[41] A striking feature is the plethora of names by which he is known. There is, for example, the term "Satan," which is a proper noun and the equivalent of the common noun "devil." In addition, Matthew also refers to him as the "Tempter" (4:3), "Beelzebul" (12:24, 27), the "Evil One" (13:19), and the "Enemy" (13:39).

Matthew describes Satan, in his opposition to the kingdom, as one whose power is exceeded only by God and Jesus themselves. Thus, Matthew attributes to Satan a "kingdom" (12:26), which means that he, too, is looked upon as one who rules in the universe. Moreover, under his control are such supernatural beings as "angels" (cf. 25:41) and "demons,"[42] or "unclean spirits" (cf. 10:1). Of course, he also enjoys the fealty of humans (cf. 13:38c), and a major way in which he brings his power to bear upon them is through temptation: he endeavors to get them to act or to live "lawlessly,"[43] that is to say, in a manner which is contrary to the will of God.[44] For this reason he is called the "Tempter" (4:3) and the "Evil One" (cf. 6:13; 13:19).

Since Matthew shows that the kingdom of heaven draws near to people in the person of Jesus Messiah, the Son of God, it is not surprising that in the First Gospel Jesus himself should be the primary target of Satan. Indeed, the first time Satan is directly mentioned is in connection with his desire to tempt Jesus to disobedience and hence to the forfeiture of his divine sonship (4:1–11). In this confrontation, however, Jesus proves himself to be superior to Satan (cf. 4:4, 7, 10–11). But although defeated by Jesus, Satan continues to wield power in the world. As a result, both the kingdom of heaven and the kingdom of Satan possess in the First Gospel the quality of "already . . . but not yet," though with opposite tendencies: on the one hand, Satan has already been overcome by the power of the kingdom of heaven at work in Jesus, but his capacity for evil has not yet been taken from him; on the other hand, the kingdom of heaven has already entered the world in Jesus the Son so as to challenge the rule of Satan, but it has not yet been established in splendor to Satan's destruction and the total elimination of evil.

The clash between Satan and Jesus Son of God in the First Gospel is an ongoing one. Satan is characterized as "the strong man" and Jesus Son of God, in that he casts out demons by the Holy Spirit and brings people into the sphere of God's reign, as the one who "binds" him and "plunders his goods" (12:28–29; cf. 8:29). Conversely, Satan and those who do his bidding are depicted as doing violence to the kingdom of heaven and as "plundering" it (11:12). A case in point is Satan's enlistment of Peter in an effort to put Jesus at cross-purposes with his Father and to turn him away from the path that leads to the cross (16:21–23). It is precisely to fend off onslaughts of Satan such as this that Jesus teaches his disciples to pray (6:13): "And lead us not into temptation, but deliver us from the Evil One." On another level, Satan also exercises his malevolent will against Jesus through the Israelite crowds[45] and their leaders,[46] who ask Jesus for a sign or who put him to the test, not the least while he is hanging on the cross (27:39–43). Indeed, through a parable of Jesus, Matthew makes the programmatic observation that Satan is the personal "Enemy" of Jesus Messiah, who has usurped in Israel the allegiance that is due Jesus alone (13:24–30). Nevertheless, as the story of the temptation at the beginning of the Gospel adumbrates, the repeated attacks of Satan are not sufficient to induce Jesus to divest himself of this divine sonship and to bring him from his mission (cf. 16:21).

As the arch-adversary of Jesus Messiah, the Son of God, it follows that Satan should be portrayed, also in post-Easter times, as endeavoring to bring people under his influence. Thus, whereas the exalted Jesus is said to be active in the world to raise up "sons of the kingdom," Satan is active in the world to raise up "sons of the Evil One" (13:37–39). The mark of Satan's followers is contrariety to the will of God, or "lawlessness" (*anomia*; 13:41). At the consummation of the age they will be cast into the "fiery furnace" (13:40, 42). Indeed, at the Last Judgment the exalted Jesus will finally consign Satan, his angels, and his "sons" to "eternal punishment" (25:41, 46).

But the church, too, must face in post-Easter times the onslaughts of Satan, who would destroy it. Externally, Satan attempts this through the persecution and affliction of the church by Jews and gentiles.[47] Still, he is active inside the church as well. For example, Satan subverts the influence of the "word of the kingdom" upon persons who join the church but are without "understanding," or true faith, and so brings them under his sway. In Matthew's eyes, however, the fatal sign of those who serve Satan is that they are "lawless."[48] Such lawlessness comes to expression in any number of ways, such as in false speech (cf. 5:37), in a failure to be loving (cf. 20:15) or to be single-mindedly devoted to God (cf. 6:23), in lukewarmness toward the demands of discipleship (cf. 25:26), in an unwillingness to forgive a fellow-disciple (cf. 18:32, 35), and in sins of every kind against the second table of the law (cf. 15:19).

There is one circle within the church, however, to which Matthew calls special attention in warning his community against lawlessness, the so-called false prophets.[49] The false prophets appear to be enthusiasts,[50] but the thing to note is that Matthew compares them to "rapacious wolves" (7:15) whose deeds are evil, or "lawless,"[51] and who lead many astray (24:11, 24). At the last, they will be denied entrance to the consummated kingdom of heaven (7:21, 23).

In sum, therefore, Matthew's Gospel evinces a remarkable degree of dualism in its description of the kingdom of heaven and of the kingdom of Satan. The antagonists, Jesus and Satan, are locked in mortal combat, and the power of each is cosmic in scope, extending both to supernatural beings and to the world of humankind. At the same time, Jesus in his messianic ministry has in effect already defeated Satan, so that even though he can wreak havoc on the church, bringing disciples to fall, and raise up in the world those who will do his bidding, he cannot, finally, prevail. In the present time the power of the kingdom, which the exalted Son of God already wields, serves to strengthen the disciples in their struggle with Satan, and at the last, when the kingdom of heaven will be consummated in splendor, the exalted Jesus will judge Satan and cast him and all who are his into the eternal fire.

The Kingdom of Heaven and
Israel and the Nations

It has just been shown that Matthew views the nearness of the kingdom of heaven as a mortal threat to the rule of Satan. At the same time, because Matthew likewise holds that Satan is at work in both Israel and the world to effect his malevolent purposes, the kingdom of heaven must, as he sees it, establish itself on earth in the face of concerted opposition from both Jews and gentiles.

Matthew is eminently concerned, it will be recalled, to affirm that Jesus Messiah, the Son of God, in whom the kingdom of heaven draws near to humankind, is sent first of all to Israel.[52] Through his ministry in Galilee of teaching, preaching, and healing,[53] Jesus confronts Israel with the kingdom. Israel's response, however, is one of repudiation. It does not perceive who he is (cf. 11:25; 13:13), and the leaders put him to the test,[54] demand from him a sign,[55] accuse him of blasphemy[56] and of breaking the law,[57] and charge him with carrying out his ministry on the authority of the prince of demons (9:34; 12:24). Hence, the whole of Israel proves itself to be "an evil and adulterous generation"[58] that refuses to repent and receive the kingdom of heaven.[59]

The finality with which Israel rejects its Messiah and therefore the kingdom of heaven comes to light in the passion narrative. The animosity of the leaders of the people against Jesus is such that they plot his death and see to it that it takes place.[60] To this end, they secure the aid of Judas,[61] of the crowds,[62] and of the gentile authorities.[63] In the presence of Pilate and at the foot of the cross, however, the crowds join their leaders in total condemnation of Jesus (cf. 27:15–26). Together, these two groups function, ironically, as the acknowledged representatives of that people God had once chosen to be his own.[64] Finally, in regard to the Easter event, although the truth of the matter is that God has raised Jesus from the dead, the Jews perpetuate the slanderous rumor that his disciples came by night and made off with his body (28:11-15).

Accordingly, Matthew depicts Jesus Messiah, the Son of God, as bringing the kingdom to his people Israel in his person and ministry and as being repudiated by them. In addition, in looking back upon the years since Easter, Matthew can boast of no change in Israel's attitude toward Jesus. Indeed, in these years his church has been forced to separate itself from the Jewish community. Two indications of this in the Gospel are the related circumstances that Matthew describes the synagogues Jesus visits as "their synagogues"[65] and treats the leaders of the people, whether "chief priests and elders" or "scribes and Pharisees" or "Pharisees and Sadducees," as though they had always formed as monolithic a front as do the leaders of the Pharisaic Judaism his church must face.

In charting the course of the recent past, therefore, Matthew shows that if Israel did not receive Jesus' proclamation of the gospel of the kingdom,[66] neither has it received the church's proclamation of the gospel of the kingdom.[67] As can be seen from the example of its leaders, Israel steadfastly refuses to "enter . . . the kingdom of heaven."[68] What is more, Israel has even responded to the missionary efforts of the church with persecution.[69] Thus, disciples of Jesus, particularly "missionaries," are made to submit to such ill-treatment as verbal abuse (cf. 5:11), arraignment for disturbing the peace (cf. 10:17), perjured testimony in court (cf. 5:11), flogging in the local synagogue,[70] stoning (cf. 21:35), pursuit from city to city,[71] and even death.[72] In consideration of all this, Matthew employs parables of Jesus to decry Israel under all of the following images: it is as unreceptive "soil" in which the seed of proclamation is unable to take root and bear fruit and so dies (cf. 13:3b-7); it is as "weeds" ("darnel") that are sown by the enemy of the farmer who sows good seed (cf. 13:24-30); it is as a "son" who does not repent of his duplicity toward his father and do his will (cf. 21:28-32); it is as "farmers" who lease a vineyard but refuse to pay rent and not only beat, kill, and stone the owner's slaves but murder his son as well (cf. 21:33-41); and it is as "guests" who are invited by a king to a wedding celebration for his son but make light of the invitation and seize, abuse, and kill the slaves of the king (cf. 22:1-8).

As for the leadership of Israel, Matthew is vitriolic in his condemnation of it. The Matthean Jesus denounces the "scribes and Pharisees" as "hypocrites" (cf. chap. 23)[73] and charges them with all of the following: not only do they refuse to "enter" the kingdom themselves, but they also prevent others from "entering" it (cf. 23:13); they search out proselytes only to make of each one a "son of Gehenna" twice as much as themselves (cf. 23:15); they are blind guides who teach people to swear falsely (cf. 23:16–22); they concern themselves with trivia, neglecting the weightier matters of the law (cf. 23:23–24); outwardly they appear "clean" to people, but inwardly they are full of extortion (cf. 23:25–26); to others they seem right-eous, but in reality they are full of hypocrisy and lawlessness (cf. 23:27–28); while paying tribute to the prophets of old, they put to death and perse-cute those whom God sends to enlighten them (cf. 23:29–36); they esteem their own tradition of the elders more than the law of God (cf. 15:1–9); and they espouse an evil teaching of which one must beware (cf. 16:6, 11–12).

Finally, Matthew also attempts in his Gospel to answer the question of how it could ever happen that Israel should become so blind and perverse. The one answer he gives has already been noted: Israel has fallen under the rule of Satan. A second answer is that God has ordained that Israel should not be made privy to the secrets of the kingdom of heaven, for which reason the people are "blind, deaf, and without understanding."[74] In the case of both of these answers, however, one should observe that there is no intention on the part of Matthew to excuse Israel for its repudiation of Jesus and its persecution of the church. Quite the opposite, Matthew goes to great lengths to underline the guilt that devolves upon Israel for its failure to receive its Messiah: all Israel makes itself juridically responsible for the blood of Jesus (27:25); the leaders of the people themselves announce the punishment and loss that the nation must endure for its treat-ment of the Son of God (21:37–41); and in words of Jesus, Matthew also declares that Israel is furthermore culpable for its mistreatment of Chris-tian missionaries (23:34–36).

What, then, has resulted from Israel's fateful response? One result has been the destruction of Jerusalem (cf. 22:7). But this is only the physical manifestation of a second result, namely, that God, as Matthew puts it in a saying of Jesus, has chosen to "take away" his kingdom from Israel and to "give it" to a "nation" which will "produce the fruits of it" (21:43). This "nation," of course, is the "church,"[75] and the "kingdom" is the rule of God as a present reality.[76] Consequently, owing to Israel's rejection of the proclamation of the gospel of the kingdom by Jesus and by his ambassadors, God withdraws his rule from Israel and Israel ceases to be his chosen people.

Yet a third result of Israel's response is that the basic mission of Matthew's church is no longer to Israel per se (chap. 10) but to the nations.[77] Christian missionaries are, as has been observed, still at work in contemporary Israel,[78] but it is on the gentiles that the Matthean church has now set its sights. Still and all, Matthew is under no illusions as to the reception the nations will give the gospel of the kingdom and the church's missionaries. Already in his day he reports in words of Jesus that disciples bear witness to the gentiles even as they are "dragged before governors and kings" (10:18), that the church is "hated by all the nations" because of its allegiance to Jesus,[79] that it suffers "tribulation" at the hands of gentile opponents,[80] and that members of the church are "killed."[81] In view of such happenings as these, it is little wonder that Matthew should see Satan at work in the world raising up "sons of the Evil One" (13:38–39) or that he should boldly state through the mouth of Jesus that also the nations, because of the way they have treated those who belong to the church,[82] will undergo judgment at the consummation of the age.[83]

To recapitulate, Matthew describes the kingdom of heaven as confronting Israel in the person of Jesus Messiah, the Son of God, and, following his death and resurrection, in the church's proclamation of the gospel of the kingdom. Israel, however, has responded negatively both to Jesus and, since Easter, to his church's missionary efforts. The upshot is that God has withdrawn his rule from Israel and now exercises it in Jesus, the exalted Son of God, in the "empirical" sphere of the church. Israel, on the other hand, stands condemned, and the mission of the church is henceforth to proclaim the gospel of the kingdom, not solely to Israel, but to all the nations. At the same time, the nations, too, are hostile to the message of the church, and Matthew warns that at the latter day they will likewise have to answer to the exalted Jesus. But until that day, the task of the church is indeed to proclaim the gospel of the kingdom everywhere, and through this proclamation, in the face of opposition from Jew and gentile, God in Jesus, and in association with the church, visits people with his gracious rule.

With this summary, we have reached the point where Matthew's understanding of the church becomes important. This, then, is the topic of the final chapter.

CHAPTER FOUR

MATTHEW'S UNDERSTANDING OF THE COMMUNITY OF DISCIPLES

Because Israel has repudiated its Messiah, God, claims Matthew, has withdrawn his kingdom from it and given it to the church (21:43). The church, as the central thought of the Gospel defines it, is the community in which God in the person of his Son Jesus chooses to dwell to the end of the age ("God [is] with us").[1] More specifically, this community is made up of those who, since Easter, have been called by Jesus through baptism to be his disciples (28:19). In contrast to Israel and the gentiles, the church is the new "nation" God has raised up for himself (21:43), the "people" whom Jesus has saved from their sins (1:21). Within the flow of the gospel-story, the disciples who follow Jesus are, both positively and by reverse example, "typical" of the members of Matthew's church. It is, therefore, by analyzing Matthew's portrait of the disciples that one gains insight into his understanding of the church.

The Nature of Discipleship

A distinctive feature of Matthew's portrait of Jesus is the unique relationship he enjoys with God (cf. 11:25–27). God is the Father of Jesus in a way not predicated to other human beings.[2] Conversely, Jesus is the Son of God in a manner that is true of no one else.[3] Nevertheless, when Jesus calls persons to follow him and therefore to become his disciples, Matthew shows that through him, the Messiah Son of God, they enter into a relationship of sonship with God.

So it is that Jesus designates his disciples in the First Gospel as "sons of God" (5:9), "sons of your heavenly Father" (5:45), and "sons of the kingdom" (13:38). By the same token, when speaking of God to the disciples, Jesus repeatedly refers to him as "your Father"[4] and even exhorts them to address him as "Father" in prayer (6:9). With an eye to himself, Jesus declares that his disciples are his true relatives (12:49) and his "brothers" (28:10), and tells the disciples that they, too, are all "brothers."[5] In one passage in the Gospel, Matthew has Jesus stress at once his uniqueness in comparison with his disciples and his "relatedness" to them: "For whoever does the will of *my Father* in heaven is *my brother, and sister, and mother*" (12:50).

Matthew is at pains throughout his Gospel to emphasize in scenes that depict Jesus as interacting with his disciples both the uniqueness of Jesus as the Son of God and his close association with his disciples as sons of God and brothers. On the one hand, Jesus stands out from his disciples as the obvious figure of authority. The relationship he has with them is characterized as that of "teacher and learner," of "master and slave" (10:24–25). They regularly address him as "Lord," acknowledging thereby his exalted station and divine authority.[6] Moreover, it is he who summons, dispatches, commands, and teaches, and it is they who follow, go, obey, and heed.

For example, Jesus bids his first disciples to come after him, and they leave their nets at once and follow him.[7] He ascends the mountain to teach, and they come to him as he sits (5:1–2). He embarks into the boat, and they step in after him.[8] He summons the twelve for missionary instruction, and they attend to his words.[9] He takes the lead in going through the grain fields, and they walk with him (12:1). He enters the house, and they approach him and hear the explanation of the parable of the tares (13:36). He gives the permission, and Peter walks on the water (14:28–29). He dispatches the two disciples, and they return with the animals on which he rides into Jerusalem (21:1–7). He determines where he will eat the passover, and they make the necessary preparations (26:18–19). He tells the woman after he has been raised where his disciples are to meet him, and the disciples go to the mountain in Galilee to which he has directed them (28:10, 16).

On the other hand, Matthew also highlights the close association the disciples have with Jesus. Recently, Hubert Frankemölle has called attention to the importance in the First Gospel of the concept of "being with Jesus."[10] The Greek preposition translated as "with" (*meta* + genitive case) is frequently employed to denote accompaniment (cf., e.g., 12:3: "David . . . and those who were 'with him'"). Of great interest is the way in which Matthew carefully restricts the circle of those who share in the presence, or the company, of Jesus. Thus, if one takes the Second Gospel for purposes of comparison, one discovers that Mark depicts a broad spectrum of people as sharing in the company of Jesus: not only are Peter, James, and John[11] or the twelve[12] or the disciples[13] said to be "with Jesus" or he "with them," but it is also said, respectively, that Jesus eats "with sinners and toll collectors" (2:16), that other boats are "with him" as he journeys across the lake (4:36), that the demoniac whom he heals begs to be "with him" (5:18), that Jesus accedes to the plea of Jairus and goes "with him" to his sick daughter (5:22–24), and that Judas at the last supper eats "with me [Jesus]" (14:18).

In contrast to Mark, Matthew's presentation of those said to be "with Jesus" or Jesus "with them" is far more limited in scope. Except for Mary his mother (2:11) and toll collectors and sinners (9:11), the list extends only to Peter,[14] one of Jesus' followers (26:51), Peter and the two sons of Zebedee (26:37–38), and the twelve or eleven disciples.[15] Noticeably absent from this list are such as the crowds or their leaders or even Jairus and the healed demoniacs. Indeed, in the First Gospel Judas does not so much as eat with Jesus but merely dips his hand with him in the dish, in this manner marking himself as the one who will betray Jesus (26:23). In point of fact, Jesus is only "with Israel" as with a "faithless and perverse generation" from whom he will withdraw his presence (17:17), and the critical principle obtains: "He who is not *with me* is against me, and he who does not gather *with me* scatters" (12:30).

In the First Gospel, then, Jesus grants the privilege of his company almost without exception only to his own. Before Easter, these are his disciples. After Easter, they are his church (16:18). The disciples before Easter follow along "with Jesus" as he leads them to the cross and resurrection.[16] The church after Easter makes its way toward the consummation of the age and the parousia on the promise of the exalted Jesus that he will surely be "with them [you]" (28:20).

What such close association with Jesus means theologically Matthew explains in the key passages 1:23 ("Emmanuel . . . God [is] *with us*"), 18:20 ("there am I *in the midst of them*"), and 28:20 ("I am *with you* always"). It means, as the central thought of the Gospel also states, that through his presence Jesus Messiah, the earthly and exalted Son of God, mediates to his disciples or church the gracious, saving presence of God and his rule. Now if, in line with this truth, these three passages are examined in context, one sees that they relate the presence and therefore the authority of the earthly and exalted Son of God to the basic activities characterizing not so much the ministry of the earthly disciples as that of the post-Easter church: baptizing (28:19), teaching (28:20), prayer (18:19), church discipline (18:18), and, in general, the mission to the nations (28:19). In addition, Matthew likewise reveals that the church's celebration of the Last Supper is done not only in commemoration of the shedding of the blood of the Son of God for the forgiveness of sins,[17] but also in anticipation of that day to come when he will again drink wine "with them [you]" in the glorious kingdom of his Father (26:29). In short, Matthew utilizes the concept of "being with Jesus" and the related idiom of his "being with them" in order to restrict close association with Jesus almost exclusively to the circle of his disciples and, theologically, to set forth the truth that the church worships and carries out its ministry to the close of the age in the presence and on the authority of the exalted Son of God, through whom God exercises his gracious, saving rule.

The Will of God

Accordingly, the disciples, in being called by Jesus to walk in his presence, become the recipients of divine grace (4:17-22). They are the "blessed" ones (5:3-11), those who are given to share in that unique religious joy that is indicative of the eschatological age of salvation which God's drawing near in his Son has inaugurated. They are the ones declared to be the "salt of the earth" (5:13) and the "light of the world" (5:14). As such, they follow along behind Jesus, and he imparts to them his teaching (cf. 5:1b-2). They for their part respond to the gracious call of Jesus and to his teaching by leading lives that reflect the "greater righteousness" (5:20).

The teaching of Jesus has to do, as was observed in chapter 2, with the will of God in terms of its original intention.[18] This teaching is binding on the church for all time to come, and the church discharges its own ministry of teaching in post-Easter times by rehearsing all that Jesus has commanded (28:20).

To speak of the will of God is to broach the question of Matthew's understanding of the law. For purposes of clarification, it should be noted that the term "law" *(nomos),* when used by itself in the First Gospel,[19] does not refer merely to the Ten Commandments but, more broadly, to the five books of Moses, or the Pentateuch. Similarly, the expression "the law and the prophets" denotes quite simply the whole of the OT as it was known to the church of Matthew and functioned for it as scripture.[20]

Now Jesus is in Matthew's eyes, as has oft been said, the Messiah, the Son of God, and what he teaches, as was just recalled, is the will of God in terms of its original intention. How, then, does Jesus' teaching square with the Mosaic law? One place where this comes to light is in the antitheses of the Sermon on the Mount (5:21-48). The antitheses are those peculiar sayings of Jesus that are characterized by some variation of the formula "You have heard that it was said to the men of old : . . but I say to you . . ." (5:21-22, 27-28, 31-32, 33-34, 38-39, 43-44).

Commentators do not agree on how to construe the antitheses. On one fundamental matter they divide themselves into two camps. On the one hand, some hold that Jesus in the antitheses only deepens, intensifies, or radicalizes at points the intention of the law of Moses.[21] On the other hand, others contend that, in certain of the antitheses, Jesus radicalizes the intention of the law of Moses to such a degree that he abrogates it.[22]

To review the antitheses, scholars seem to agree that the first and second ones, on murder (5:21-26) and on adultery (5:27-30), merely intensify commands of Moses.[23] Moreover, a majority is likewise convinced that the sixth antithesis, on love of one's enemy (5:43-48), is also intended simply to intensify a command of Moses (cf. Lev. 19:18). As for the fifth antithesis, on retribution (5:38-42), those scholars who take the position that Jesus in certain of the antitheses so radicalizes the law of Moses that he abrogates it all appear to agree that such is the case here. For whereas the Mosaic law regulates retribution but in so doing makes provisions for it,[24] Jesus, they maintain, forbids it altogether. This leaves the third and fourth antitheses. What is to be made of them?

John Meier argues in a technical treatment of Matthew 5 that these antitheses, too, are to be seen as abrogating Mosaic injunctions.[25] With respect to the third antithesis (5:31-32), Jesus rescinds the permission for divorce that Deut. 24:1-4 presupposes and, in line with this, likewise annuls the command about the giving of the bill of divorce. The so-called exceptive clause of 5:32 ("except on the grounds of *porneias*") allows for divorce, not by reason of "unchastity" (as the RSV, e.g., translates *porneias*), but only in the event two people (e.g., gentiles joining the church) have, in violation of Lev. 18:6-18, entered into what must be judged to be an "incestuous marriage." So understood, the third antithesis does not provide a "loophole" for easy divorce (namely, adultery), but, on the contrary, is thoroughly radical in its prohibition of divorce.

Concerning the fourth antithesis (5:33–37), what Jesus revokes is the permission the law grants, as well as the obligation it in some instances enjoins, to make use of vows and oaths.[26] The thrust of this antithesis is that vows and oaths are wrong because they infringe upon the majesty of God: he who is holy and ever truthful is made the guarantor of the alleged truth of sinful human beings.

Consequently, it would seem that the Matthean Jesus, in the fifth antithesis for sure, and very likely in the third and fourth antitheses as well, does abrogate parts of the Mosaic law in the interest of promulgating more stringent injunctions. But if this is the case, how does abrogation of parts of the Mosaic law harmonize with the words of Jesus in 5:17–18, where he announces that he has "not come to abolish the law or the prophets . . . but to fulfill them," and that "till heaven and earth pass away, not an iota [yod], not a dot [stroke], will pass from the law"?

The answer, it appears, is that Matthew, as 11:13 indicates, sees the law and the prophets, the entire OT, as "prophesying," as pointing forward, to the events that mark the eschatological age of salvation. At the center of these events, of course, is Jesus Messiah, the Son of God. With his coming, in what he says and does, the law and the prophets attain to their "fulfillment" (5:17). The law that remains in force as long as heaven and earth shall last (5:18) is the law precisely as Jesus delivers it to his disciples and church. It is, properly understood, the messianic law. For none other than Jesus Messiah is the one who teaches the "way of God" with absolute truth and authority[27] and hence stands above Moses: "You have heard . . . but I say to you." It is exactly his words that the church is to hear and do (7:24–27), and these words will never pass away (24:35). In brief, if for the Jews Moses is the supreme arbiter of the will of God, for the church it is Jesus Messiah, the Son of God. Accordingly, the law as Jesus has given it is what has abiding validity for the members of Matthew's community.

Matthew's twofold concern that, on the one hand, Jesus should not be thought of as an enemy of the Mosaic law but that, on the other, it is his word that transcends the word of Moses comes to the fore elsewhere in the Gospel. For example, the pericope on divorce and celibacy (19:3–12) reinforces the point of the third antithesis in the Sermon on the Mount (5:31–32): except in the case of the incestuous marriage, divorce is forbidden.[28]

In this pericope, too, Matthew pictures Jesus as pitting himself against Moses: "Moses permitted you to divorce your wives . . . but I say to you . . ." (19:8-9). And the fact that Jesus' injunction is indeed radical, even to the point of revoking Mosaic law in order to transcend it, is evident from the disciples' observation and Jesus' reply to them: the disciples assert, "If such is the case of a man with his wife, it is not expedient to marry" (19:10); and Jesus counters, "Not all men can receive this precept . . ." (19:11).

But in other pericopes having to do with the Mosaic law, Matthew portrays Jesus as making his point without at the same time overturning a command of Moses. Thus, in the stories on plucking grain on the sabbath (12:1-8) and on healing the withered hand (12:9-14), Jesus in both instances suppresses the sabbath law in favor of the law of love (12:7, 12). At the same time, he does not declare the sabbath law void,[29] and the passage 24:20 is indication that Matthew's church observed this law as long as it did not conflict with its ministry of love. In the pericope on clean and unclean (cf. 15:10-20a), Jesus does not, as Mark explains it in his version of the story (cf. 7:19), rescind the dietary laws laid down in Leviticus 11 and Deuteronomy 14. Instead, without at all passing judgment on the question of defilement through outward things such as foods, Jesus in Matthew's account speaks to the issue of the defilement that is of the heart (15:18).

If according to Matthew Jesus upholds the Mosaic law and yet revokes it at points in the interest of more radical precepts, the same can be said of the attitude he takes toward the so-called tradition of the elders. This tradition, cultivated by Pharisaic Judaism, was oral in form. It consisted of a vast number of regulations, regarded as obligatory for the individual Jew, the purpose of which was to apply the law of Moses to new times and new circumstances. To return to the pericope on clean and unclean (15:1-20), Matthew depicts the Pharisees and scribes as approaching Jesus with the charge that his disciples, because they eat with unwashed hands, are transgressing the tradition of the elders (15:1-2). Later, in private conversation, Jesus tells his disciples that this requirement is not binding on them. "To eat with unwashed hands," he declares flatly, "does not defile a man" (15:20).

In this instance, then, Jesus authoritatively sets aside a stipulated ritual of the tradition of the elders. What is more, in 16:11-12 he warns his disciples to "beware . . . of the teaching of the Pharisees and Sadducees," and in chapter 23 he employs bitter sarcasm in attacking their regulations (cf. also 15:6). On the other hand, in 23:2–3 Matthew describes Jesus as telling the disciples that the "scribes and the Pharisees sit on Moses' seat, so practice and observe whatever they tell you," and in 23:23 Jesus even speaks approvingly of the Pharisaic rule concerning the tithing of "mint and dill and cumin" ("but these things one ought to have done"). On balance, therefore, it seems that the position the church of Matthew takes toward the Pharisaic tradition of the elders is that it complies with it, at least to some undetermined extent, but not if it contravenes the will of God as Jesus has articulated it. The word of Jesus is, again, what is normative for the church.

Although the church of Matthew adheres to the law as Jesus has given it and, to some extent, also to the tradition of the elders, this should not be taken to mean that the mark of its piety is consequently the development of an elaborate system of casuistry. In a number of passages, the Matthean Jesus makes it eminently clear that the deepest intention of the will of God is love. This has already been encountered in the twin pericopes on plucking grain on the sabbath[30] and on healing the withered hand,[31] for in both the sabbath law is suppressed in favor of the law of love. But Matthew furthermore has Jesus state this programmatically: in the so-called golden rule in the Sermon on the Mount (7:12); in his statement at 23:23 on the "weightier matters of the law" ("justice," *"mercy,"* and "faithfulness"); and in the pericopes on the rich young man (19:19) and on the great commandment (22:34–40).

To consider the latter unit, Jesus announces that all the law and the prophets hang on two commandments: "You shall love the Lord your God with all your heart, and with all your soul, and with all your mind" (cf. Deut. 6:5); and "You shall love your neighbor as yourself" (cf. Lev. 19:18). As Matthew conceives of these words of Jesus, the idea is not that these commandments are the greatest ones because they are to be valued more highly than the others and hence are to be observed in some sense more diligently. Instead, the idea is that they reveal the ground, or the intention, of all the precepts of the law or, indeed, of the entire will of God as set forth in the whole of the OT (cf. "law and prophets"; 22:40). That is to say, keeping the injunctions of the law, or doing the will of God, is always, in essence, an exercise in love.

The "Greater Righteousness"

Thus far, it has been pointed out that through the call of Jesus Messiah, the Son of God, the disciples of Jesus become sons of God and brothers, those who are given to share in his company and so to live in the sphere of God's gracious rule. As they follow Jesus, he imparts to them, among other things, his teaching. The content of his teaching is the will of God, so that it is binding on the disciples and on the church for all time to come. In teaching the will of God, Jesus teaches the law, and in the process intensifies and radicalizes it even to the point where he, the Son, places himself above Moses. Whether it is a matter of the law or of the tradition of the elders, the word of Jesus, the Messiah Son of God, is consequently what is normative for the disciples and the church.

But how are the disciples to respond to the gracious call of Jesus to follow after him and to the teaching he imparts to them along the way? As Jesus puts it in the Sermon on the Mount and as has been mentioned in passing, it is with lives that reflect the "greater righteousness" (5:20). What is the meaning of this concept?

The term "righteousness" *(dikaiosynē)* occurs seven times in the First Gospel, and it appears that Matthew has not appropriated it from the tradition but has himself inserted it in each instance into the gospel materials.[32] Basically, Matthew applies it in a twofold manner. Although he alludes to the righteousness of the scribes and Pharisees (5:20), he speaks explicitly of the "righteousness of God"[33] on the one hand and of the "righteousness of the disciples"[34] on the other.

The righteousness of God is his justice, which issues in salvation and judgment for humans. Thus, for the disciples of Jesus to "hunger and thirst for righteousness" (5:6) is for them to long fervently for God to establish his just rule over all the world, a longing that, Jesus pledges, will be satisfied. Similarly, the injunction to "seek first the kingdom and his [the Father's] righteousness" (6:33) is a summons to the disciples to orient their lives toward the approaching, consummated rule of God and the end-time salvation attendant to it. Jesus exhorts the disciples to pray for this themselves in the second and third petitions of the Lord's Prayer: ". . . thy kingdom come, thy will be done, on earth as it is in heaven" (6:10).

But Matthew also predicates "righteousness" to the disciples ("your righteousness"). In this connection, the term connotes doing the will of

God, the heavenly Father,[35] or, to use a metaphor, "producing fruit."[36] For instance, for the disciples to be "persecuted on account of righteousness" (5:10) is for them to be persecuted because they lead lives pleasing to God and consonant with being in the sphere of his rule. And for them to "beware of practicing their [your] righteousness before men" (6:1) is for them to be on their guard lest they be hypocritical[37] in their piety or the conduct of their lives.

Against this background, the key passage 5:20 can again be taken up. Here the Matthean Jesus tells the disciples that "unless your righteousness exceeds that of the scribes and Pharisees, you will never enter the kingdom of heaven." As is obvious, the meaning of the term "righteousness" in this verse is likewise that of doing the will of God: the piety of the disciples is to be superior to that of the scribes and Pharisees. What does Matthew have in mind in recording this saying of Jesus?

Negatively, the point of comparing the piety of the disciples with that of the scribes and Pharisees has to do with the circumstance that Matthew pictures Jesus elsewhere in the Gospel as charging the leaders of Israel with "hypocrisy."[38] Now Jesus defines hypocrisy as saying one thing and doing another (23:3). But such duplicity is by no means a relatively small matter of little consequence. On the contrary, it is indicative of "lawlessness" *(anomia)*, of not doing the will of God and therefore of producing "rotten fruit" that will result in condemnation to Gehenna.[39] In view of this, it becomes apparent that the adjective "greater" in the expression "greater righteousness" must be pressed beyond the normal signification of the word: in reality, the righteousness that Jesus requires of the disciples in 5:20 is not simply different in degree from that of the scribes and Pharisees but, indeed, different in kind.

What the expression the "greater righteousness" signifies positively Matthew explains in the pivotal passage 5:48. This is the verse with which he concludes the entire section of the Sermon on the Mount devoted to the antitheses. In 5:48, the Matthean Jesus exhorts the disciples: "You, therefore, shall be *perfect (teleioi)*, as your heavenly Father is perfect." Deuteronomy 18:13 shows how the first half of this saying is to be understood: "You shall be *whole-hearted* [LXX: *teleios* ("perfect")] in the service of the Lord your God" (NEB). In line with this, the righteousness of the disciples is to be "greater" in the sense that they are to be single-hearted, or undivided ("whole," "complete"), in their doing of the will of God.

Matthew uses the adjective "perfect" one other time in his Gospel (19:21), in the story of the rich young man (19:16–22). This story alerts the reader once again to the proper context within which Matthew treats of the "greater righteousness." As Matthew tells it, the young man, desirous of obtaining eternal life, affirms to Jesus that he has observed all the commandments, and asks him whether there is anything he still lacks (19:16–20). In reply, Jesus remarks: "If you would be perfect [whole, complete], go, sell what you possess and give to the poor, and you will have treasure in heaven; and come, follow me" (19:21). The critical point in these words is that perfection ("wholeness," "completeness"), the reward of which is eternal life, is associated with following after Jesus. Hence, for Matthew, the proper context for doing the greater righteousness, for observing the will of God, is, quite singularly, discipleship.

Accordingly, Matthew defines the greater righteousness as doing the will of God, and he firmly associates it with discipleship. But what is the hallmark of the greater righteousness, of doing the will of God? The hallmark is, of course, love: love toward God, and love toward the neighbor (19:18–19; 22:37–39). Toward God, the disciples assume the posture of "little ones," that is, they humble themselves before God and depend upon him totally,[40] and they do the will of God as Jesus has taught it (cf. 5:2—7:29). Toward the neighbor, the disciples are the "servants" of all and not the "lords" of all,[41] the "slaves" of all and not the "bosses" ("first") of all (20:27).

In their exercise of the greater righteousness, the disciples are not without example. In fact, Matthew places them in the long train of all those in the history of salvation held to be "the righteous" *(díkaioi)*. Cases in point in the "time of Israel (OT)" are Abel (23:35), the prophets (5:10–12), the saints,[42] and the martyrs (23:35). In the "time of Jesus (earthly—exalted)," they are such as Joseph (1:19), John the Baptist (21:32), and Christian missionaries (10:41). But the foremost example is Jesus himself.

In one of the scenes of Jesus' trial before Pilate, Matthew terms Jesus in the words of Pilate's wife "that righteous man" (27:19), and by this he intends to show that Jesus is completely innocent of any wrongdoing (cf. 27:4, 24). Still, this scene merely underlines the circumstance that, in Matthew's eyes, Jesus is the one par excellence who does the will of God. This comes to the fore already in the story of the baptism (3:13–17), where Jesus, in the first words he utters in the Gospel, indicates that he submits to baptism by John, not out of need for repentance and the confession of sins as is the case with Israel,[43] but because this, too, is in accordance with the will of God (3:15). Other pericopes in the Gospel that likewise portray Jesus in a special way as the one who is perfectly obedient to the will of God are the stories of the temptation (4:1–11), of Jesus in Gethsemane (26:39, 42), and of Jesus on the cross (27:39–44). Furthermore, it is as one who himself does the will of God perfectly that Jesus also bids his disciples to pray to God, ". . . thy will be done, on earth as it is in heaven" (6:10), or announces to them that his true relatives are those who do the "will of my Father who is in heaven" (12:50), or warns them that the only ones who will ever enter the kingdom of heaven are, again, those who do the "will of my Father who is in heaven" (7:21; cf. also 18:14).

Consequently, Matthew does indeed regard Jesus Messiah, the Son of God, as the "righteous one" par excellence. As such, he is the preeminent "model" for the disciples and church of what it is to do the greater righteousness. But true as this is, it is just as true that Matthew never permits this facet of his portrait of Jesus to blur or to diminish in the slightest Jesus' uniqueness. Although the followers of Jesus are to emulate him, there is no thought in Matthew's conception of things that they can ever become his equals. The sonship and the obedience to the will of God which Matthew predicates to Jesus Messiah, he predicates to no one else.

One further matter begs for consideration. Matthew places the disciples and therefore also the members of his church in line with all "the righteous" in the history of salvation, and the exhortation they receive is that they are to do the "greater righteousness." At the same time, except for what appears to be post-Easter Christian missionaries who seem to have run the high risk of martyrdom,[44] followers of Jesus are not as a rule designated in the First Gospel as "the righteous." Instead, Matthew, as will be seen next section, reserves the predication "the righteous" for those of his contemporaries only whom the exalted Jesus will declare at the Last Judgment to have, in truth, done the will of God.[45]

The Church of Matthew

It is clear from the preceding discussion that Matthew's portrait of the church is not without its exalted features. Through the gracious summons of Jesus Messiah, the Son of God, the disciples of Jesus become sons of God and brothers, and enter into the sphere of God's kingly rule. In response to this gracious summons, the disciples reflect in their lives the greater righteousness, which is to say that they do the will of God as Jesus makes it known. In terms of Matthew's "kingdom language," it may be said of the church that here are "sons of the kingdom"[46] to whom God has "given the kingdom" (21:43), who in Jesus Son of God share the "forgiveness" of the kingdom[47] and hear and understand the "word of the kingdom,"[48] who have been "instructed about the kingdom" (13:52) and hence know the "secrets of the kingdom" (13:11), who seek the "righteousness of the kingdom" (6:33) and have been entrusted with the "keys of the kingdom" (16:19), who pray fervently for the "coming of the kingdom" (6:10) and produce the "fruits of the kingdom,"[49] and who at the consummation of the age will "enter the kingdom"[50] and "inherit" it.[51]

But despite this exalted view of the church, it is noteworthy that Matthew steadfastly refuses to identify the church with the kingdom of heaven. Instead, he associates it with the kingdom. One reason why Matthew associates, but does not identify, the church with the kingdom surely has to do with the circumstance that it is by no stretch of the imagination a pure community of the holy. On the contrary, it is a *corpus mixtum* ("mixed [disunited] body"), and one indication of this is the fact that while Matthew attributes to its members the status of being "the called" (22:14), he noticeably reserves the status of being "the elect"[52] or, as we saw, "the righteous"[53] for those members to whom the exalted Jesus will grant at the latter day "eternal life" (25:46).

In the present age, the church is caught up in the throes of the so-called messianic woes (24:8). Not only does it suffer persecution at the hands of Jews[54] and tribulation at the hands of gentiles,[55] but it is also afflicted by internal difficulties, such as the following: there are members who do "not understand" the Word of the kingdom and consequently are without true faith (13:19), or who are "false prophets" and lead other disciples astray,[56] or who surrender their faith because they cannot endure persecution or tribulation,[57] or whose lives as disciples remain sterile because their faith succumbs to the cares of the world or to the seduction of wealth (13:22), or who deny Jesus Son of God (10:33), or who despise others in the community (18:10), or betray fellow-disciples to gentile opponents (24:10), or cause other disciples to lose their faith (18:6). And there is the threat of status-seeking in the church (23:8–12), hatred among members (24:10), rampant "lawlessness" resulting in lovelessness,[58] lukewarmness toward

Christian duty (25:26), an unwillingness to forgive the neighbor (18:35), and other evil that threatens the spiritual welfare of the community (cf. 15:19).

In response to this situation in which he at once affirms the presence of God's rule in his community but must catalogue its many aberrations from the will of God, Matthew directs the attention of his church squarely to the consummation of the age *(synteleia tou aiōnos)* and the inauguration of the future kingdom by the exalted Jesus.[59] He does this in order that his community might see the present as decisively qualified by the future and recognize that the disciple pursues life only in the light of the approaching kingdom. The fact of the matter is that the God who will miraculously establish his rule "then" is even "now" at work in his Son to motivate the disciples ethically to do his will. Throughout this age, therefore, what characterizes the life of the disciple and of the church in their relation to the kingdom of heaven is this tension between present and future, which is at the same time a tension between "ethics" and "eschatology."[60]

In application of this "ethical-eschatological tension" to the life of the church, Matthew both warns and exhorts his fellow-members. Negatively, he sternly reminds them that the possession of wealth poses the most serious kind of threat to the disciple who would "enter" the future kingdom (19:23), that those who cause another disciple to lose his faith or who forfeit their own will be severely punished,[61] that the coming of the exalted Jesus for judgment will catch unawares those who are not prepared for it,[62] that those who do not do the will of God in the present can be certain that their appeals to Jesus, the Judge, at the latter day will avail them nothing (7:15-23), and that in this present age they dare never forget that the church, too, will most assuredly undergo judgment at the consummation.[63]

Positively, Matthew exhorts the members of his community to all of the following: to see their lives in the present as being shaped by God's future promises (5:3-10); to be diligent in offering their (eschatological) petitions to God, especially the prayer Jesus taught them (6:9-13); to practice a piety that is pleasing to God against that day when he will bestow upon them his eschatological "reward"[64]; to emulate in the present the Lord Jesus, Son of God, so that each one "takes up his cross and follows" him, thus "finding" his life even while "losing" it;[65] to have no fear of their enemies but to commend themselves to the providential care of the God who can condemn to Gehenna (10:28-31) and to depend upon him as completely as does a child upon his father (18:3–4); to suffer persecution with joy as ones who will inherit the kingdom (5:10–12); and to be like faithful slaves[66] who are totally committed to the doing of the will of God,[67] being ever watchful and ready in view of the unexpected coming of the exalted Jesus.[68]

In sum, as Matthew understands it, the church of Jesus, the exalted Son of God, is the eschatological people of God whose existence is characterized by a tension between the present and the future. Even now the church lives in the sphere of the gracious rule of God as exercised by Jesus and has as its commission to proclaim the gospel of the kingdom to the nations and hence to invite them, too, to enter this sphere. But though the church lives under God's rule, it is in no wise immune to the forces of evil. On the contrary, it is exposed in the present to the so-called messianic woes. Severely afflicted as it is from within and without, Matthew calls the church to see its present situation in the light of the future kingdom of heaven. In this way, the members of the community, through eschatological warning and exhortation, are brought face to face in the present with the God of the future kingdom who would, through his Son, motivate them ethically to do his will and so be heirs of life.

The Situation of Matthew

Scholars generally associate Matthew's Gospel with the city of Antioch in Syria. As to date, they place it at about A.D. 85 or 90, reasoning that it was written some fifteen or twenty years following the destruction of Jerusalem, alluded to in 22:7, and the writing of Mark, which Matthew apparently used. To turn from the theological portrait Matthew sketches of Jesus and of the disciples, the final task is to ask as to the kind of community that stood behind the First Gospel.[69] What can be said about it as a sociological entity?

The language the Matthean community spoke was almost certainly Greek. This is indicated already by the quality of the language of the First Gospel. It is not what may be termed "translation Greek," the secondary rendering, for example, of a Hebrew or Aramaic original. Seemingly, Matthew placed Mark, itself written in Greek, at the basis of his Gospel, and also made use of Q, which likewise came to him in Greek. In a test of the language of the First Gospel, C. F. D. Moule states that although Matthew betrays a feeling for "Semitic atmosphere" and has at times taken over Semitisms from his sources or even given a phrase a Semitic twist himself (cf., e.g., 7:28; 11:1; 13:53; 19:1; 26:1: *"And it happened* when Jesus finished . . ."), he can be seen on the whole to have been "an educated person commanding sound Greek with a considerable vocabulary."[70]

If one judges from the contents of the Gospel, the members of the Matthean community were of both Jewish and gentile background. Features of the Gospel that suggest that Matthew wrote for a sizeable Jewish-Christian constituency are numerous. For one thing, Matthew utilizes key terms that are Jewish in tone. The sanctified life of the disciple, for example, is known as "righteousness."[71] The preferred designation for the rule of God is "the kingdom of heaven" instead of "the kingdom of God," which is the expression Mark and Luke employ. God is often referred to as "your heavenly Father" or as "your Father who is in heaven" (cf. the Sermon on the Mount) and the disciples of Jesus as "sons of God" (5:9), "sons of your Father who is in heaven" (5:45), or "sons of the kingdom" (13:38). The end of time and the final day are termed, respectively, "the consummation of the age"[72] and "the day of judgment."[73] These are but a sampling of Matthew's penchant for "Jewish-like" phraseology.

The Matthean picture of Jesus is likewise Jewish in hue. He is the "Son of Abraham," the one in whom the entire history of Israel reaches its culmination (1:1–17). He is furthermore the "Messiah,"[74] or "Coming One,"[75] who has been sent specifically to the "lost sheep from the house of Israel" (15:24). He is also the "Son of David," the royal figure who stands in the line of David,[76] the "King of Israel [the Jews]" who suffers on behalf of his people (chap. 27). Indeed, Jesus is, in sum, the "Son of God," or "Emmanuel," the eschatological "shepherd" in whom God, in fulfillment of OT prophecy, has drawn near to dwell with his people to the end of the age[77] and who will, in fulfillment of the "Son-of-man" prophecy of Daniel, return to judge all humankind (25:31–46).

The ministry of Jesus, too, has a particularly Jewish aura about it. Matthew is at pains to show that it takes place almost exclusively within the confines of Israel (cf. 15:24; also 10:6). Except for his fateful journey to Jerusalem (19:1), Galilee is the place of Jesus' activity,[78] especially the environs of Capernaum,[79] which is "his own city" (9:1) where he "dwells" (4:13) and may have a "house."[80] Thus, it is *from* Galilee that the news of Jesus spreads throughout all Syria (4:24), and it is *to* Galilee that the crowds from the Decapolis, Jerusalem, Judea, and across the Jordan come to be with him (4:25). When Jesus leaves Galilee, it is only briefly.[81] In fact, on one occasion when he withdraws into the regions of Tyre and Sidon, it appears that he merely crosses the border, for it is said of the Canaanite woman that she "came out" toward Jesus (15:21-28).

Until Easter, the disciples in the First Gospel also share in Jesus' concentration on Israel. Matthew devotes the whole of the section 9:35—10:42 to their projected mission to Israel, which goes beyond anything one finds in either Mark or Luke.

The attitude Jesus takes toward the law and the tradition of the elders likewise suggests that Matthew wrote for a strong Jewish-Christian constituency. Although Matthew depicts Jesus as abrogating at points both the law and the tradition of the elders,[82] he also depicts him as upholding both to the extent that they do not conflict with his teaching of the will of God.[83] The Marcan Jesus, by contrast, appears to overthrow the legal system of the Jews (cf. 7:1-23).

Finally, the manner in which Matthew treats certain other details is yet another factor that points to the Jewishness of a large segment of his community. Unlike Mark, Matthew does not, for instance, explain such Jewish regulations as the washing of hands before meals,[84] and neither does he explain the custom of wearing amulets and tassels (23:5). Semitic words, while translated at times (cf. "Emmanuel," 1:23; "Golgotha," 27:33; cry of dereliction, 27:46) are at other times left untranslated (cf. *'hraka,"* 5:22; *"Beelzeboul,"* 10:25; *"korbanan,"* 27:6), and it is furthermore assumed that the readers will be familiar with a peculiarly Jewish turn of phrase (cf., e.g., "straining out the gnat," 23:24; "whitewashed tombs," 23:37).

But if the unmistakable Jewishness of much of the First Gospel favors the thesis that Matthew wrote it with a sizeable Jewish-Christian constituency in mind, the attitude he takes toward the mission to the nations shows that there were also Christians in his community of gentile origin. One looks in vain in the First Gospel for traces of the fierce controversy surrounding the gentile mission which are so prominent in Paul (Galatians 2) and Acts (chap. 15). On the contrary, one can detect in the First Gospel from beginning to end a pronounced "gentile bias."

Already in the genealogy of Jesus, four non-Israelite women are listed as the ancestors of Jesus ("Tamar," "Rahab," "Ruth," and "the wife of Uriah" [Bathsheba]; 1:3, 5-6). In chapter 2, the "magi from the East" are described as "worshiping" Jesus and presenting him gifts (vv. 1-2, 11). Jesus' settling in "Galilee of the gentiles" to begin his ministry to Israel prefigures the post-Easter return of the disciples to Galilee, from where they will undertake their mission to the nations.[85] As the second of a series of ten miracles, Jesus heals the servant of a centurion, and attendant to this he declares: "Truly, I say to you, not even in Israel have I found such faith; I tell you, many will come from east and west and sit at table with Abraham, Isaac, and Jacob in the kingdom of heaven" (8:5–13). At 12:21, Matthew quotes from the OT in order to proclaim Jesus as the one in whom the "gentiles will hope," and at 13:38 he writes that it is in the "world" that "sons of the kingdom" will be raised up. In the parables of the wicked husbandmen (21:33–46) and of the great supper (22:1–14), Matthew employs figurative speech to depict the influx of gentiles into the church (21:41; 22:9–10), and, more directly, he has Jesus announce in 24:14 and 26:13 that it is throughout the entire world that the gospel of the kingdom will be proclaimed. Last, the circumstance that Matthew in a saying of Jesus can also designate the church as a "nation" (21:43) further goes to prove that his community has in fact surmounted the problem of the mission to the nations and that increasingly gentiles are joining its ranks.

A church with members of Jewish and gentile origin, the Matthean community was "urban" and prosperous as well. In comparison with Mark, who uses the word "city" *(polis)* eight times and the word "village" *(kōmē)* seven times, Matthew uses the word "village" only four times but the word "city" no fewer than twenty-six times. The latter statistic is all the more striking when it is observed that several occurrences of the word "city" seem to relate to circumstances in Matthew's own time.[86] Perhaps, then, the Matthean church was a "city church."[87]

The evidence that Matthew's church was also well-to-do is strong. The Lucan Jesus, for example, pronounces a blessing on "the poor" (6:20) but the Matthean Jesus on "the poor in spirit" (5:3). The Marcan Jesus commands the disciples in conjunction with their missionary journey to take with them no "copper coin," that is, small change (6:8), but the Matthean Jesus commands them to take no "gold, nor silver, nor copper coin" (10:9). The Lucan Jesus tells a parable about "minas" (19:11–27) but the Matthean Jesus about "talents" (25:14–30), one of the latter being worth approximately fifty times as much as one of the former. The Lucan Jesus says in the words of the householder in the parable of the great supper: "Go out quickly to the streets and lanes of the city, and bring in the poor and maimed and blind and lame" (14:21); but the Matthean Jesus simply says in his version of these words: "Go therefore to the thoroughfares, and invite to the marriage feast as many as you find" (22:9). And in Mark (15:43) and Luke (23:50–51), Joseph of Arimathea is a member of the council who is looking for the kingdom of God, but in Matthew he is a "rich man . . . who also was a disciple of Jesus" (27:57).

It seems, in fact, that the community behind the First Gospel was well accustomed to dealing in a wide range of money. Whereas Luke mentions "silver" and a few kinds of money[88] and Mark mentions an assortment of what on the whole were the lesser denominations, Matthew makes no reference whatever to the *lepton,* the smallest unit of money cited in the Gospels (a small copper coin = c. ⅛ cent), but does refer to all of the following: the *kodrantēs* ("quadrans" = c. ¼ cent), the *assarion* ("assarion" = c. 1 cent), the *dēnarion* ("denarius" = c. 18 cents), the *didrachmon* ("double drachma" = c. 36 cents), the *statēr* ("stater" = c. 80 cents), the *talanton* ("talent" = c. $1,080), and to *chalkos* ("copper coin"), *argyrion* ("silver"), *argyros* ("silver"), and *chrysos* ("gold"). Indeed, if one takes the three terms "silver," "gold," and "talent," one discovers that they occur in the First Gospel no fewer than twenty-eight times, which may be compared with the single use of the word "silver" by Mark and the fourfold use of it by Luke. Against a background of wealth such as these terms indicate, it makes sense that Matthew should have appropriated Mark's warning against riches in 13:22 (Mark 4:19) and sharpened the saying of Jesus at 19:23 so that difficulty in entering the kingdom is predicated, not merely to "those who have means" (Mark 10:23), but to the "rich man." In light of the preceding, it looks, again, as though the Matthean community was in no sense materially disadvantaged.

Accordingly, from what can be discerned the church of Matthew, firmly established by the last decade of the first century, was a Greek-speaking community of people of Jewish and gentile origin which was rather well-to-do and situated in or near a city, most likely Antioch of Syria. Now it furthermore seems, as was noted above in passing, that the social and religious climate in which this community found itself was one of intense conflict. On the one hand, it appears that these Christians were living in close proximity to hostile pagans. Whether or not their mission to the nations was the sole reason, Matthew speaks of them as being hauled into court by gentile authorities, judicially harassed ("handed over to tribulation"), hated "by all," and even put to death.[89] Clearly, Matthew depicts members of his church as enduring persecution from the side of their gentile neighbors.[90]

But it likewise appears that the Matthean church was living in close proximity to a vigorous Jewish community. The evidence for this is multiple. For instance, the parable of the tares (13:24–30) may refer to this directly, for it is possibly in regard to the church's relationship to Israel that Matthew reports Jesus as saying, "Let both grow side by side until the harvest" (13:30).[91] In a similar vein, if the story of the payment of the temple tax (17:24–27) can be interpreted to mean that the Jewish Christians in Matthew's community were being encouraged, despite their "freedom," not to offend Jews by refusing to participate in the collection of contributions throughout Jewry in support of the Patriarchy at Jamnia,[92] then this unit, too, may speak for close contact between Jews and the church of Matthew.

Perhaps Matthew's presentation of Jesus, of the disciples, and of the leaders of the Jews also gives indication that the Matthean church lived in close proximity to Jews. Thus, it may secondarily have been with an eye to the Jews about him that Matthew portrays Jesus Son of God as the ideal Israelite (cf., e.g., 4:1–11) and elevates him above Moses as the supreme teacher of the will of God (cf. the Sermon on the Mount). In addition, Matthew's description of Christian piety as the righteousness that is "greater" than that of the scribes and Pharisees may also have had the Jews "next door" in mind (5:20), and this could further be the case for the many invectives that are hurled at the Jewish leaders throughout the Gospel (chap. 23). On another level, although the essential task of the church in the time of Matthew was unquestionably to make disciples of the nations (28:18–20), this does not mean, as was mentioned earlier, that no missionary activity whatever was being done among Jews. The missionary discourse of chapter 10, which has to do with evangelization especially among Jews though also among gentiles (vv. 17–18, 22–23), was not without relevance for the church of Matthew, and the passage 23:34 is an unmistakable reference to missionary activity among the Jews which, seemingly, was taking place in Matthew's day. The church's mission to the Jews has not met with success and its task henceforth is to go to the gentiles, but continued work among the Jews points to no lack of interaction between Matthew's church and the Jewish community.

Still, if Matthew's church lived in close proximity to a strong Jewish community, it is not to be thought of as a "splinter group" that was nevertheless a member of the Jewish league of synagogues.[93] The place of Matthew's church is no longer within Judaism but without it. Several factors compel this conclusion.

To begin with, Matthew, more rigorously than either Mark or Luke, makes of Jesus and his disciples a group set apart from the Israelite crowds and their leaders. This comes to the fore already in the way in which Matthew has persons address Jesus and develops his ecclesiological concept of "being with Jesus." As for the latter, it was observed at the outset of this chapter that Matthew very carefully reserves for the disciples alone the privilege of sharing in the company, or presence, of Jesus, so that it is not said of Judas or of the crowds or of the Israelite leaders that they are "with Jesus" or that he is "with them." Correlatively, Matthew distinguishes sharply, as was also seen, between the manner in which the disciples and persons without faith approach Jesus: whereas the disciples address him as "Lord," opponents and persons without faith address him only as "rabbi" or "teacher." The "apartness" of Jesus and his disciples in the First Gospel reflects, it would seem, the religious distance that separated the Matthean church from the Jewish community.

Matthew's use of the expression "their [your] synagogue(s)," his massive apology against Israel as an institution, and the apparent organizational autonomy of his community are further indications that his church was no longer tied to Judaism. To take the last point first, Matthew's community was, as will be seen, not at all under Jewish religious control but had its own form of organization that dealt with such weighty matters as those of doctrine and of church order. In addition, by regularly appending the modifying genitive "your" or "their" to the noun "synagogue(s),"[94] Matthew attests idiomatically to the disassociation of his community from Judaism. Also, except to acknowledge that the "scribes and the Pharisees are seated on the chair of Moses" (23:2), Matthew has virtually nothing good to say of Israel as a religious institution. Typically, there is no "friendly scribe" in the First Gospel as there is in the Second of whom it is written: "And when Jesus saw that he answered wisely, he said to him, 'You are not far from the kingdom of God'" (Mark 12:34). On the contrary, the one scribe in the First Gospel who requests of Jesus that he become his disciple is turned away with the words: "Foxes have holes, and birds of the air nests, but the Son of man has nowhere to lay his head" (8:20).[95] Indeed, far from evincing affinity for contemporary Israel, Matthew, as noted last chapter, mounts a massive apology against it. As far as he was concerned, contemporary Israel was, as a saying of Jesus puts it, a "plant which my heavenly Father has not planted [and] will be rooted up"

(15:13). And if Matthew's church did not escape the persecution of gentiles, the persecution it endured at the hands of contemporary Israel was, as has been seen, equally severe and even more widespread.[96]

Consequently, the Matthean community, a church with members of Jewish and gentile background which stood outside the orbit of official Judaism but lived in close proximity to both Jews and gentiles, encountered from without persecution on the part of both Jew and gentile. What is to be said of the internal structure of the community?

Called through baptism to follow Jesus, the risen and exalted Son of God who presides over and resides in his church,[97] the Christians of Matthew's community knew themselves to be "sons of God"[98] and "brothers" of Jesus and of one another.[99] As sons of God, they were also "little ones," for they recognized their total dependency upon their heavenly Father.[100] As brothers of Jesus and of one another, they were at the same time "servants" and "slaves" of one another (20:25–28). And as followers of Jesus, they were likewise "disciples" (*mathētai*; cf., e.g., 8:23), for they had taken upon themselves his yoke and they "learned" from him.[101] Internally, therefore, the Matthean community may be described as a brotherhood of the sons of God and the disciples of Jesus.

Within this brotherhood, two or three groups can perhaps be distinguished. One group was that of the "prophets" (10:41; 23:34). In principle, Matthew looked upon his entire community as standing in the tradition of the OT prophets and the twelve disciples of Jesus (5:12; 13:17). It appears, however, that there were also Christians in his own time who were specifically regarded as "prophets." They are described in the Gospel as itinerant missionaries who proclaim the gospel of the kingdom to Jews[102] but especially to gentiles.[103]

Whether these Christian prophets functioned exclusively beyond the Matthean community is difficult to say. In 7:15–20, Matthew seems to allude to prophets who plainly were active within his community. At the same time, he denounces them in the passage as "false," as "ravenous wolves . . . who come to you in sheep's clothing" (7:15). What is more, they were enthusiasts, for it is said that in the name of Christ they prophesy, cast out demons, and perform many miracles (7:22). Their works, however, are castigated as contravening their profession of the name of Christ (7:16–20). The result is that Matthew condemns them in words of Jesus as "workers of lawlessness" whom the exalted Jesus at the latter day will banish from his presence (7:23). The point is, is one to infer from Matthew's references to these false prophets who were at work within his community and against whom he polemicizes so vigorously that, conversely, the legitimate Christian prophets, too, are to be thought of as carrying out a ministry not only as missionaries beyond the community but also as preachers of the gospel of the kingdom within the community? One can only conjecture.

One or possibly two groups within the Matthean community have been identified: the "prophets" and the "false prophets." Another identifiable group is those who functioned as teachers. They are designated variously. Thus, the term "righteous man" (dikaios; 10:41) denotes a teacher of righteousness,[104] and the terms "rabbi" (hrabbi; 23:8), "scribe" (grammateus; 23:34), and "wise man" (sophos; 23:34) most likely refer without distinction to persons who are expert in matters pertaining to the scriptures and the law.[105] The verses 10:41 and 23:34, in which three of these four terms occur, show that Christian teachers, too, served as missionaries to the Jews, perhaps conversing or debating with them about the meaning of the scriptures, the law, and the traditions in the light of the coming of Jesus Messiah.

But these Christians who served as teachers were likewise active within the community, as can be presupposed from the passage 23:8–12 (cf. also 13:52). What their exact competences were is hard to know. Still, at one point this question becomes acute, because it touches on the matter of the regulation of the life of the community.

By Matthew's time, his church had already developed a structure for governing communal life. In 16:19, for example, Peter receives from Jesus the promise of the power of the "keys of the kingdom of heaven." He receives this promise, however, in his capacity as the "first" of the disciples to be called[106] and therefore as the one who is their "spokesman" and who is "typical" of them and of later Christians.[107] Peter's "primacy," therefore, is not that of being elevated to a station above the other disciples but is "salvation-historical" in nature: he is, again, the "first" disciple whom Jesus called to follow him. Since Peter is the first among the disciples all of whom have been called and are in this sense equal, the power of the keys Jesus promises him is perhaps best equated with the power of "binding and loosing," which the other disciples exercise as well as he (cf. 16:19 with 18:18). The power of "binding and loosing," in turn, pertains to the regulation of church doctrine and discipline.[108] Accordingly, whatever the particular contribution of those who served as teachers, it was the entire Matthean community that decided the matters of doctrine and discipline. As the passage 18:18-20 indicates, this community made such decisions gathered together in the name and hence in the presence and on the authority of the exalted Son of God. Moreover, as it did so, it was conscious of the fact that the touchstone of whatever it decided was that it must be in keeping with the injunction given by Jesus to "observe all that I have commanded you" (28:20).

The Matthean community, then, was without a peculiar "teaching office" such as contemporary Judaism was in the process of developing. Indeed, with an eye toward those engaged in teaching, Matthew is explicit about the problem of position and status. This is reflected by the circumstance that the Matthean Jesus expressly forbids them to arrogate to themselves a station that would set them above the rest of the community. They are not, for example, to assume the title of "rabbi" or "teacher," for these titles are the prerogative of Jesus Messiah, the Son of God (23:8, 10). Neither are they to assume the title of "Father," for this title is the prerogative of God himself (23:9). They are to be the opposite of the "scribes and Pharisees" in contemporary Judaism, who have office and authority but "shut the kingdom of heaven against men," neither entering themselves nor allowing those who would enter to go in (23:13). On the contrary, in the church "all . . . are brothers" (23:8), and the eschatological maxim applies that "whoever exalts himself will be humbled, and whoever humbles himself will be exalted" (23:12).

A word is in order about Matthew himself, the author of the First Gospel. In greatest measure, scholarly opinion does not identify Matthew the author with Matthew the apostle. One reason is that if Matthew is dependent upon Mark, as most scholars believe, it is difficult to explain how it could happen that the apostle Matthew, an eyewitness of the ministry of Jesus, should have taken the greater part of his Gospel from Mark, whom no one claims was a disciple or eyewitness of Jesus. Another reason is that the theological outlook of the writer of the Gospel seems to be that of the second, not the first, generation of Christians to follow Jesus. One might also ask, if it is correct that the Gospel was written about A.D. 85 or 90, whether the apostle Matthew could reasonably be expected to have lived long enough to write this book.

It could be, however, that the apostle Matthew, although not the author of the First Gospel, was associated at one time with the church that stood behind it and was esteemed as a founder or "patron disciple." This would explain why the story of the call of Matthew (9:9) substitutes in the First Gospel for the story of the call of Levi (cf. Mark 2:14; Luke 5:27), and why the list of the disciples of Jesus has been adjusted accordingly (cf. 10:3 ["Matthew the tax collector"] with Mark 3:18 and Luke 6:15).

Still, some scholars, while they agree that Matthew the apostle did not write the First Gospel, nevertheless hold that his association with it was more direct than this. Appealing to a notice of the second-century Church Father Papias, which reads that "Matthew wrote [collected] the oracles [accounts] in the Hebrew language and every one interpreted them as he was able,"[109] they contend that Matthew the apostle was the author of a primitive Aramaic document that was subsequently taken up into the First Gospel. In its various forms, this thesis has been thoroughly debated over the years, but the results have been inconclusive.

Can, then, Matthew the author be identified? The answer is no. It is sometimes suggested that the First Gospel was produced, not by an individual, but by a school.[110] Most scholars, however, prefer to think in terms of individual authorship. A few argue that the Gospel was written by a gentile Christian, basing their case on the author's alleged "distance" from Judaism, on his use of the LXX and treatment of certain Semitic words and other terms, and on the supposed relationship within the Gospel between tradition (= Jewish Christian) and redaction (= gentile Christian).[111] But by far the majority of scholars regard the author as a Christian of Jewish background, and they point to many of his theological emphases and to the architechtonic structure of his work as proof that he had enjoyed rabbinical training. Perhaps, therefore, Matthew the author can best be described as a Greek-speaking Jewish Christian of the second generation after Christ who possessed a universal missionary outlook and had most probably enjoyed rabbinical training.

To conclude, the church of Matthew, by the last two decades of the first century A.D., must be regarded as a firmly established community. Greek was its language, and the constituency was of both Jewish and gentile origin. It was furthermore "urban" and well-to-do, located perhaps in or near Syrian Antioch, and its neighbors were Jews and gentiles. The atmosphere in which it lived was one of conflict, both from within and from without. From without, it encountered gentile but especially Jewish persecution. From within, it was troubled by miracle-working false prophets, among others. Still, this community, having had its ties with contemporary Judaism severed, conceived of itself as the brotherhood of the sons of God and of the disciples of Jesus. It knew the exalted Son of God to reside in its midst, and it traced its teaching and ethics to him. Groups within the community can be distinguished, but hierarchical tendencies were resisted. There were, for example, the itinerant prophets, who proclaimed the gospel of the kingdom among Jews and gentiles, although the fundamental mission of the community was to the latter. And there were those engaged in teaching, who, although they, too, undertook missionary activity, instructed the community in the will of God as taught by Jesus. But whatever the contribution of the latter, when it came to making final decisions concerning matters of doctrine and church discipline, it was the entire community, under the aegis of the exalted Son of God, that decided.

Matthew, the author of the First Gospel, lived within this community. On behalf of his fellow believers and to meet their needs, he proclaimed in written form the gospel of the kingdom. In so doing, he held up to them Jesus Messiah, the Son of God, as the savior of all humankind, and, in relation to Jesus, he spoke of God the Father and of what it meant to be Jesus' disciple. Although Matthew so recedes behind his document that he can scarcely be known, his gift to the church universal is one in which people in every age are called to "life."

NOTES

(Works listed in the Selected Bibliography or referred to more than once in a single chapter are cited by name and title only.)

Chapter One

1. Cf. T. Zahn, *Das Evangelium des Matthäus* (Kommentar zum Neuen Testament I; 3d ed.; Leipzig: A. Deichert, 1910); also A. Schlatter, *Der Evangelist Matthäus* (5th ed.; Stuttgart: Calwer, 1959). Although his understanding of Matthean priority is not the same as that of Zahn and Schlatter, one might also point in this connection to the commentary by M.-J. Lagrange: *Évangile selon Saint Matthieu* (7th ed.; Paris: J. Gabalda, 1948).

2. Cf., e.g., Zahn, *Das Evangelium des Matthäus*, 42–43.

3. Cf. ibid., 154–59.

4. Cf. Matt. 9:10, 28; 13:1, 36; 17:25.

5. Cf. Matt. 4:21; 17:1; 20:20, 24; 26:37.

6. To identify historically the man called "Matthew" in 9:9 and 10:3 is complicated by the fact that the same story that is told of him in the First Gospel is told in Mark 2:14 of one who is called "Levi."

7. Cf. Matt. 4:17; 16:21; 26:16.

8. Cf. Matt. 11:25; 12:1; 14:1.

9. Cf. Matt. 8:13; 10:19; 18:1; 26:55.

10. Cf. Matt. 9:22; 15:28; 17:18.

11. Cf. Matt. 13:1; 22:23.

12. Cf. Matt. 4:8; 5:1; 14:23; 15:29; 17:1; 24:3; 28:16.

13. Cf. Matt. 4:23; 9:35; 12:9; 13:54.

14. Cf. Matt. 9:10, 28; 13:1, 36; 17:25.

15. Cf. Matt. 4:21; 12:15; also 9:9, 27; 11:1; 12:9; 13:53; 14:13; 15:21, 29; 19:15.

16. Cf. Mark 9:5; 10:51; 11:21; 4:38; 9:17, 38; 10:35; 13:1.

17. Cf. Matt. 26:25, 49; 8:19; 12:38; 19:16; 22:16, 24, 36.

18. Cf., e.g., Matt. 8:2, 6, 8, 21, 25; 9:28.

19. Cf. Mark 4:13; 6:52; 8:17, 21; 9:10, 32.

20. Luke 9:45; 18:34; 24; John 2:22; 12:16; 16:4.

21. Cf. Matt. 13:11, 16–17; also 13:23, 51.

22. Cf. Matt. 13:36 with 13:51; 15:15–16 (note the word "still" in v. 16); 16:9 with 16:12.

23. Cf., e.g., K. L. Schmidt, "Die Stellung der Evangelien in der allgemeinen Literaturgeschichte," *Eucharistērion*, ed. H. Schmidt (*Festschrift* H. Gunkel; Göttingen: Vandenhoeck & Ruprecht, 1923), 50–134; the same, *Euangelion* (Nachdruck der Ausgabe Gütersloh 1927 and 1931; Darmstadt: Wissenschaftliche Buchgesellschaft, 1970) I–II; E. Hennecke, *New Testament Apocrypha*, ed. W. Schneemelcher, trans. R. McL. Wilson (London: Lutterworth, 1963) I, 75–80; R. Bultmann, *The History of the Synoptic Tradition*, trans. J. Marsch (Oxford: Basil Blackwell, 1963), 368–74.

24. Bultmann, *History of the Synoptic Tradition*, 373–74.

25. Ibid.

26. Ibid., 371–72.

27. Cf. M. J. Suggs, "Gospel, Genre," *The Interpreter's Dictionary of the Bible: Supplementary Volume*, ed. K. Crim, et al (Nashville: Abingdon, 1976), 370.

28. Ibid., 371.

29. Ibid., 370.

30. G. N. Stanton, "The Gospel Traditions and Early Christological Reflection," *Christ, Faith and History*, eds. S. W. Sykes and J. P. Clayton (Cambridge: Cambridge University Press, 1972), 197.

31. Ibid., 198–99.

32. Cf. C. W. Votaw, *The Gospels and Contemporary Biographies in the Greco-Roman World* (Facet Books; Philadelphia: Fortress Press, 1970), 2–5, 11.

33. Cf. M. Hadas and M. Smith, *Heroes and Gods* (Religious Perspectives 13; New York: Harper & Row, 1965), 3–9, 57–66, 101–4. Cf. also Suggs ("Genre," 371), who describes the Gospels as being "biography with aretalogical traits."

34. Cf. C. H. Talbert, *What Is a Gospel?* (Philadelphia: Fortress Press, 1977), 96–98.

35. Cf. W. R. Farmer (*Jesus and the Gospel* [Philadelphia: Fortress Press, 1982], 144–46), who has specifically Matthew in mind.

36. Cf. Shuler, *A Genre for the Gospels*, 92–106.

37. On this topic of Gospel genre, cf. also the remarks of N. R. Petersen, *Literary Criticism for New Testament Critics* (Guides to Biblical Scholarship; Philadelphia: Fortress Press, 1978), 44.

38. *Jesus' Proclamation of the Kingdom of God*, eds. and trans. R. H. Hiers and D. L. Holland (Lives of Jesus Series; Philadelphia: Fortress Press, 1971).

39. *The Quest of the Historical Jesus*, trans. W. Montgomery (reprint ed., New York: Macmillan, 1955).

40. As regards this phenomenon, cf., e.g., M. E. Boring, *Sayings of the Risen Jesus* (SNTSMS 46; Cambridge: Cambridge University Press, 1982); D. E. Aune, *Prophecy in Early Christianity and the Ancient Mediterranean World* (Grand Rapids: Eerdmans, 1983); G. Stanton, "Matthew as a Creative Interpreter of the Sayings of Jesus," *Das Evangelium und die Evangelien*, ed. P. Stuhlmacher (Tübingen: J. C. B. Mohr, 1983), 273–87.

41. For a summary chapter on the literary character and the theology of the gospel-source Q, cf. J. D. Kingsbury, *Jesus Christ in Matthew, Mark, and Luke*, Proclamation Commentaries (Philadelphia: Fortress Press, 1981), chap. 1.

42. Not all scholars, however, agree that Mark was the first of the four canonical Gospels. Perhaps the most influential work contesting this view is that of W. R. Farmer, *The Synoptic Problem* (reprint ed., Dillsboro, N.C.: Western North Carolina Press, 1976).

43. For a literary-critical treatment of Matthew, which also includes an introductory discussion of method, cf. Kingsbury, *Matthew as Story*.

44. For a literary-theoretical discussion of narrative criticism, cf. S. Chatman, *Story and Discourse* (Ithaca, N.Y.: Cornell Univ. Press, 1978); also D. Rhoads, "Narrative Criticism and the Gospel of Mark," *Journal of the American Academy of Religion*, 50 (1982): 411–34.

45. Cf. B. W. Bacon, *Studies in Matthew* (London: Constable, 1930), 82, 265–335.

46. Cf. Waetjen, *Origin and Destiny of Humanness*, chap. 2.

47. Cf. G. D. Kilpatrick, *The Origins of the Gospel According to St. Matthew* (Oxford: Clarendon Press, 1946), 135–37.

48. Cf., e.g., G. Schille, "Bemerkungen zur Formgeschichte des Evangeliums. II. Das Evangelium des Matthäus als Katechismus," *New Testament Studies* 4 (1957/58): 113; J. L. McKenzie, "The Gospel According to Matthew," *Jerome Biblical Commentary*, eds. R. E. Brown, J. A. Fitzmyer, and R. E. Murphy (Englewood Cliffs, N.J.: Prentice Hall, 1968), 62–64.

49. Cf. Stendahl, *The School of St. Matthew*, 24–27, 29, 35.

50. Cf. W. Marxsen, *Introduction to the New Testament*, trans. G. Buswell (Philadelphia: Fortress Press, 1968), 151–52.

51. Cf. N. Perrin, *The New Testament: An Introduction* (New York: Harcourt Brace Jovanovich, 1974), 174–77.

52. Cf. W. Trilling, *Das wahre Israel* (StANT X; 3d ed.; München: Kösel, 1964), 95–96, 162, 213.

53. Cf. H. Frankemölle, *Jahwebund und Kirche Christi* (NTAbh 10; Münster: Aschendorff, 1974), 118–19, 142, 219–20, 257–61, 319–21, 358, 384–400.

54. Cf. R. Hummel, *Die Auseinandersetzung zwischen Kirche und Judentum im Matthäusevangelium* (BEvT 33; München: Kaiser, 1963), 66–75, 162–73.

55. Cf. G. Strecker, *Der Weg der Gerechtigkeit* (FRLANT 82; Göttingen: Vandenhoeck & Ruprecht, 1962), 45–49, 184–88.

56. Cf. R. Walker, *Die Heilsgeschichte im ersten Evangelium* (FRLANT 91; Göttingen: Vandenhoeck & Ruprecht, 1967), 114–15.

57. Cf. W. G. Thompson, "An Historical Perspective in the Gospel of Matthew," *Journal of Biblical Literature* 93 (1974): 244, 252–54, 262.

58. Cf. Meier, *Vision of Matthew*, chap. 2.

59. Cf. A. Wikenhauser, *New Testament Introduction*, trans. J. Cunningham (reprint ed.; New York: Herder & Herder, 1965), 223.

60. Cf. W. G. Kümmel, *Introduction to the New Testament*, trans. H. C. Kee (Nashville: Abingdon Press, 1975), 57–61.

61. Cf. Matt. 5:1-2; 23:8-10; 28:20.
62. Cf. Mark 10:47-48; also 12:35, 37.
63. Cf. Mark 7:28; 10:51; 11:3.
64. Cf. Matt. 5:10-12; 10:17, 23, 28; 23:34.
65. Cf., e.g., Matt. 6:1, 4, 6, 18, 33; 13:49-50; 18:35.
66. Cf., e.g., Matt. 1:22-23; 2:15, 17-18, 23; 4:14-16; 8:17; 12:17-21; 13:14-15, 35; 21:4-5; 27:9-10.
67. Cf. Matthew 5—7; 10; 11; 13; 18; 23; 24—25.
68. Cf., e.g., Matt. 21:1-9 [4-5] with Mark 11:1-10.
69. Cf. note 67.
70. Cf., e.g., Matt. 8:1-4 with Mark 1:40-45; Matt. 9:17 with Mark 2:22; Matt. 12:1-21 with Mark 2:23—3:12; Matt. 10:2-5a with Mark 3:13-19a.
71. Cf. Matt. 4:8; 5:1; 14:23; 15:29; 17:1; 24:3; 28:16.
72. Cf., e.g., Matt. 2:4; 21:23; 26:3, 47; 27:1.
73. Cf. Matt. 11:5c-6; 13:19, 23; 24:14.
74. Cf. Matt. 11:5 and Luke 7:22.
75. Cf. Mark 8:38; 9:1; 13:24-27; 14:62.
76. Cf. Mark 1:15; 8:35; 10:29; 13:10; 14:9.
77. Cf., e.g., Mark 1:1, 14-15; 8:29; 14:61; 15:32, 39; 16:6.
78. On the structure of Matthew's Gospel, cf. Kingsbury, *Matthew: Structure, Christology, Kingdom*, chap. 1; and Bauer, "The Structure of Matthew's Gospel."
79. Cf. Matt. 1:1—4:16, esp. 1:1, 22-23; 2:15; 3:17; 4:3, 6.
80. Cf. Matt. 4:23; 9:35; 11:1; 11:2—16:20 (esp. 11:6; 13:57).
81. Cf. Matt. 16:21; 17:22-23; 20:17-19; 26:2.
82. Cf. also Matt. 11:27; 21:37-38, 42; 27:54; 28:5-6.
83. Cf. note 66.
84. Cf. Matt. 4:17, 23; 9:35; 15:24.
85. Cf. Matt. 24:14; 26:13; 28:19-20.

Chapter Two

1. Bornkamm ("End-Expectation and Church in Matthew," *Tradition and Interpretation in Matthew*, 32-33) and E. Schweizer (*Matthäus und seine Gemeinde* [SBS 71; Stuttgart: KBW Verlag, 1974], 65) speak on this point for numerous commentators when they write, respectively: "in only a few passages does Matthew's Gospel reveal any theological reflections on the relation of these titles of honor to each other; in the first place he is satisfied with the evidence that they are all based on Scripture"; "To be sure, with Matthew neither the ecclesiology nor the christology has been systematically thought through; therefore one should not wonder if statements stand side by side which are not in complete accord with one another."
2. Cf. Matt. 2:23; 21:11; 26:71.
3. Cf. Matt. 9:10, 28; 13:1, 36; 17:25.
4. Cf., e.g., Rom. 1:1; 5:6, 8.
5. Cf. Matt. 1:1, 18 with 1:16; 16:21 with 16:20.
6. Cf., e.g., Lev. 4:3; 6:22; 1 Sam. 12:3; 16:13; Lam. 4:20.
7. Cf. Ps. 105:15; 1 Chron. 16:22.

8. Cf., e.g., Matt. 3:3.
9. Cf., e.g., Matt. 2:17.
10. Cf. Matt. 16:13-14; 21:11, 46.
11. Cf. Matt. 9:34; 12:24; 27:63.
12. Cf. Matt. 1:16; 16:20; 24:5.
13. Cf. Matt. 1:1, 16, 17, 20, 25.
14. Cf. Matt. 1:21; 3:11; 11:3, 6.
15. Cf. Matt. 27:11, 17, 22, 29, 37.
16. Cf. Matt. 26:63, 68 and 27:41-42.
17. Cf. Matt. 1:6, 20, 25; 21:9.
18. Cf. Matt. 3:2, 6, 11.
19. Cf. Matt. 1:23; 4:17, 23; 9:35; 12:28; 21:37-38; 24:14; 28:18b-20.
20. Cf. Matt. 1:16, 18, 20.
21. Cf. Matt. 2:8-9, 11, 13-14, 20-21; 3:11.
22. Cf. Matt. 1:21, 23, 25.
23. Cf. Matt. 4:18-22; 5:9, 45.
24. Cf., e.g., Matt. 10:32-33; 12:50; 16:17.
25. Cf., e.g., Matt. 5:16, 45, 48.
26. Cf. Matt. 5:21-22, 27-28, 31-32, 33-34, 38-39, 43-44.
27. Cf. Matt. 4:17; cf. also 4:23; 9:35; 11:1.
28. Cf. Matt. 5:2, 17-18, 21-22, 27-28, 31-32, 33-34, 38-39, 43-44; 19:7-9.
29. Cf. Matt. 19:4b, 7-8 with Mark 10:3b-6.
30. Cf. Matt. 23:3, 13, 15, 16, 23, 25, 27, 29.
31. Cf. Matt. 15:14; 23:16, 24.
32. Cf. Matt. 9:13; 12:7; 22:34-40.
33. For a detailed analysis of this section of the Gospel, cf. Kingsbury, *The Parables of Jesus in Matthew 13*, chaps. 2—6.
34. Cf. Matt. 13:1-3 with Mark 4:1-2.
35. For studies of the miracles of Jesus in the First Gospel, cf. Held, "Matthew as Interpreter of the Miracle Stories," *Tradition and Interpretation in Matthew*, 165-299; Gerhardsson, *The Mighty Acts of Jesus According to Matthew*.
36. Cf. Matt. 8:5-10, 23-27; 9:2-8, 20-22, 27-31; 14:22-33; 15:21-28.
37. Cf. Matt. 12:22-30 with Mark 3:22-27.
38. Cf. Matt. 12:38 with 12:9-37; 16:1.
39. Cf. J. D. Kingsbury, "Observations on the 'Miracle Chapters' of Matthew 8—9," *The Catholic Biblical Quarterly* 40 (1978): 559-73; also Matt. 8:1, 10, 18-22, 23; 9:9, 19, 27.
40. Cf. Matt. 11:20, 21, 23; 13:54, 58; 14:2.
41. Cf. Matt. 1:23; 18:20; 28:18-20.
42. Cf. Matt. 12:10-13, 15, 22; 14:14; 15:29-31; 17:14-18; 19:2; 21:14.
43. Cf. Matt. 4:3, 6 with 4:8; 14:23 with 14:33; 17:1 with 17:5; 28:16 with 28:19.
44. Cf. Matt. 4:24-25; 9:31; 11:2, 4; 14:1.
45. Cf. Matt. 2:3; 3:7-12; also 9:34 with 9:27-30; 10:5-42.
46. It is to "forewarn" the reader that Jesus will take evasive action in the face

of danger prior to the coming of his "hour" (cf. 14:13—16:20) that Matthew reports in 12:14–15, as he also does here in 14:13, that Jesus "departed from there."

47. Cf. Matt. 14:13, 22, 34; 15:21, 29 (33), 39; 16:4c–5, 13.

48. By juxtaposing the pericope on the Gadarene demoniacs (8:28–34) with this pericope on the stilling of the storm (8:23–27), Matthew communicates to the reader "in advance" what the answer to the disciples' question is (cf. 8:29 with 8:27).

49. Cf. Matt. 2:17; 11:13; 13:17.

50. Cf. Matt. 18:6, 10, 20, 21–22.

51. Cf. Matt. 19:10–12, 13–15; 19:23—20:16; 20:20–28.

52. Cf. Matt. 21:23–27; 22:15–46.

53. Cf. Matt. 21:28—22:14.

54. Cf. Matt. 21:13; 23:38; 26:61; 27:51.

55. On the passion of Jesus in Matthew's Gospel, cf. Senior, *The Passion of Jesus in the Gospel of Matthew*; Witherup, "The Cross of Jesus: A Literary-Critical Study of Matthew 27."

56. Cf. Matt. 27:11, 29, 37, 42.

57. Cf. Matt. 27:18, 23–24, 26, 37.

58. Cf. Matt. 28:6–7, 10, 17.

59. Cf. Matt. 14:33; 16:16.

60. Cf. Matt. 16:21–22; also 17:10–13.

61. On Matthew's understanding of Jesus as the Son of David, cf. Kingsbury, *Matthew: Structure, Christology, Kingdom*, 99–103; also "The Title 'Son of David' in Matthew's Gospel," *Journal of Biblical Literature* 95 (1976): 591–602. The relevant passages are Matt. 1:1, 16, 18–25; 9:27; 12:23; 15:22; 20:30–31; 21:9, 15; 22:41–46.

62. Cf. Matt. 1:16, 20–21, 25.

63. Cf., e.g., G. Strecker, *Der Weg der Gerechtigkeit* (FRLANT 82; Göttingen: Vandenhoeck & Ruprecht, 1962), 118–20, 123–26; W. Trilling, *Das wahre Israel* (StANT 10; 3d ed.; München: Kösel, 1964), 21–51; H. Frankemölle, *Jahwebund und Kirche Christi* (NTAbh 10; Münster: Aschendorff, 1974), 80, 89, 144, 377, 398.

64. Cf., e.g., Matt. 4:7, 10; 5:33; 9:38; 11:25; 21:9, 42; 22:37; 23:39; 27:10; 28:2.

65. On Matthew's use of *kyrios*, cf. Kingsbury, *Matthew: Structure, Christology, Kingdom*, 103–13.

66. Cf. Matt. 1:18, 20, 23; 2:15; 3:17; 11:27; 17:5; 21:37–38, 42; 26:28; 27:51, 54; 28:5–6, 18–20.

67. Cf. Matt. 22:43–45 (16:22).

68. Cf. Matt. 9:28; 15:22, 25, 27; 20:30–31, 33; 21:3.

69. Cf. Matt. 14:28, 30; 17:4.

70. Cf. Matt. 7:21–22; 12:8; 24:42; 25:37, 44.

71. On recent trends in Son-of-man research, cf. B. Lindars, *Jesus Son of Man* (London: SPCK, 1983), chap. 1. On Matthew's use of "the Son of man," cf. J. D. Kingsbury, "The Figure of Jesus in Matthew's Story: A Literary-Critical Probe,"

Journal for the Study of the New Testament 21 (1984): 22–32; also "The Figure of Jesus in Matthew's Story: A Rejoinder to David Hill," *Journal for the Study of the New Testament* 25 (1985): 68–74.

72. Cf. Matt. 8:20; 9:6; 11:19; 12:8; 13:37; 16:13.

73. Cf. Matt. 12:40; 17:9, 12, 22; 20:18, 28; 26:2, 24, 45.

74. Cf. Matt. 10:23; 13:41; 16:27–28; 19:28; 24:27, 30, 37, 39, 44; 25:31; 26:64.

75. Cf. Matt. 12:40; 13:41–43; 16:27; 24:29–31, 37–39; 25:31; 26:24, 64.

76. Cf. Matt. 3:17; 4:3, 6 (27:40); 12:23 (22:42, 45); 14:33; 16:16; 24:5; 26:63–64; 27:11, 37, 42, 54.

77. Cf. Matt. 8:20 with 8:18; 9:6 with 9:8 (also 9:2); 11:19 with 11:7 and 11:16.

78. Cf. Matt. 8:20 with 8:19; 9:6 with 9:3; 12:8 with 12:2; 12:32 with 12:24; 12:40 with 12:38.

79. Cf. Matt. 12:22–37 with 9:34 and 27:63.

80. Cf. Matt. 21:11, 46.

81. In 4:17—16:20: cf. 8:20 with 8:18; 10:23 with 10:5; 12:8 with 12:1; 13:41 with 13:36; 16:13.

82. On this point, see also the remarks of G. Vermes, *Jesus and the World of Judaism* (Philadelphia: Fortress Press, 1984), 98–99.

83. Cf. Matt. 8:18, 20; 9:6, 8; 11:7, 19.

84. Cf. Matt. 9:3, 6; also 8:19–20.

85. Cf. Matt. 12:2, 8, 24, 32.

86. Cf. Matt. 26:2, 24–25, 45–46.

87. Cf. Matt. 17:22; also 17:12.

88. Cf. Matt. 10:23; 13:41–43; 16:27–28; 19:28; 24:27, 30–31, 37–39, 44; 25:31–32; 26:64.

89. Cf. Matt. 3:17; 14:33; 16:16; 17:5; 26:63–64; 27:54.

Chapter Three

1. Cf. Matt. 3:2; 4:17; 10:7.

2. Cf. Matt. 4:23; 9:35; 24:14; 26:13.

3. Cf. Exod. 15:18; Deut. 33:5; Pss. 47:2; 93:1; 96:10; 103:19; 145:13.

4. Cf. Matt. 5:17–20; 6:10, 33; 11:25–27; 12:50; 16:19; 18:18; 28:18.

5. Cf. Matt. 3:2, 11–12; 4:17; 10:7; 11:2–6; 13:16–17.

6. Cf. Matt. 5:3–10; 13:39–40, 49; 24:3; 28:20.

7. Cf. Matt. 15:24; also 2:6; 9:36; 10:6.

8. Cf. Matt. 9:15; 11:19; 22:1–10.

9. Cf. Matt. 8:11; 26:29.

10. Cf. Matt. 24:45–47.

11. Cf. Matt. 5:3–9.

12. Cf., e.g., Matt. 7:15–23; 12:45d; 13:19–21, 38–39, 49; 23:13; 24:9–11; 25:41–46.

13. Cf. Matt. 13:38; 16:16–17; 24:14; 26:13; 28:18–20.

14. Cf. Matt. 25:31–46; 13:40–43; 16:27; 24:29–31, 37–39, 44, 50.

15. Cf., e.g., Matt. 17:22–23; 20:17–19; 13:41–43; 16:28; 25:31–46.

16. Cf. Matt. 5:20; 7:21; 18:3; 19:23–24; also 23:13.

17. Cf. Matt. 18:8–9; 19:17.
18. Cf. Matt. 25:21, 23.
19. Cf. Matt. 5:20; 18:3; 23:13.
20. Cf. Matt. 8:12; 13:42, 50; 22:13; 25:30.
21. Cf. Matt. 25:6, 10.
22. Cf. Matt. 8:11; 26:29.
23. Cf. Matt. 19:30; 20:16.
24. Cf. Matt. 11:25; also 6:25–32; 10:29–30.
25. Cf. Matt. 13:11; 16:16–17.
26. Cf. Matt. 24:14; 26:13; 28:18–20.
27. Cf. Matt. 4:17; 10:7.
28. Cf. Matt. 13:47; 28:18–20.
29. Cf. Dan. 4:10–12, 21; Ezek. 31:6.
30. Cf. Matt. 4:17; 10:34–35; 11:3–6, 20; 12:41; 13:9, 43b.
31. Cf. Matt. 10:18; 24:14; also 10:14, 20, 27, 40; 23:34.
32. Cf. Matt. 4:17; 11:20; 21:31–32.
33. Cf. Matt. 13:23; 28:20.
34. Cf. Matt. 7:16–20; 12:33.
35. Cf. Matt. 6:10; 7:21; 12:50.
36. Cf. Matt. 13:43, 49; 25:37, 46.
37. Cf. Matt. 13:19, 38c–39.
38. Cf. Matt. 7:17–18; 12:33.
39. Cf. Matt. 13:42; 25:41.
40. Cf. Matt. 8:12; 13:42, 50.
41. Cf., e.g., Matt. 6:10, 13; 11:12; 12:24–29; 13:39.
42. Cf. Matt. 10:8; 12:24.
43. Cf. Matt. 7:23; 13:41; 23:28; 24:12.
44. Cf. Matt. 4:1–11; 6:13; 16:23; 27:40.
45. Cf. Matt. 11:16 (11:7); also 12:45.
46. Cf. Matt. 12:34, 38–39; 16:1; 19:3; 22:18, 35; 23:15, 28.
47. Cf. Matt. 13:39a and 5:44 with 5:10–12; 10:17–18, 22–23, 28; 23:34; 24:9.
48. Cf. Matt. 13:38c–39a, 41; 7:21–23; 24:12.
49. Cf. Matt. 7:15–23; 24:11, 24.
50. Cf. Matt. 7:22; 24:24.
51. Cf. Matt. 7:16–20, 23.
52. Cf., e.g., Matt. 2:6, 15; 10:6; 15:24.
53. Cf. Matt. 4:17, 23–25; 9:35; 11:1–6.
54. Cf. Matt. 16:1; 19:3; 22:18, 35.
55. Cf. Matt. 12:38; 16:1.
56. Cf. Matt. 9:3; also 26:65.
57. Cf. Matt. 12:10; also 12:2; 15:2.
58. Cf. Matt. 12:39–45; 16:4; also 11:16; 17:17; 23:36.
59. Cf. Matt. 4:17 and 10:7 with 11:20 and 12:41.
60. Cf. Matt. 12:14; 16:21; 21:45–46; 26—27.
61. Cf. Matt. 26:20–25, 47–50; 27:3–4.

62. Cf. Matt. 26:47; 27:20–23.
63. Cf. Matt. 27:1–2, 11–38.
64. Cf. Matt. 27:25, 39–44.
65. Cf. Matt. 4:23; 9:35; 10:17; 12:9; 13:54; also 23:34.
66. Cf. Matt. 4:23; 9:35.
67. Cf., e.g., Matthew 10; 23:34.
68. Cf. Matt. 23:13; 21:31.
69. Cf. Matt. 5:10, 12, 44; 10:17; 13:21; 23:34. For a study in depth on this theme of persecution, cf. Hare, *The Theme of Jewish Persecution of Christians in the Gospel According to St. Matthew.*
70. Cf. Matt. 10:17; 23:34.
71. Cf. Matt. 10:23; 23:34.
72. Cf. Matt. 10:28; 21:35; 23:34.
73. For a detailed study of Matthew 23, cf. Garland, *The Intention of Matthew 23.*
74. Cf. Matt. 13:10–13; also 11:25.
75. Cf. Matt. 16:18; 18:17.
76. Cf. Matt. 1:23; 18:20; 28:20.
77. Cf. Matt. 22:9; 23:37–39; 24:14; 26:13; 28:18–20.
78. Cf. Matt. 10:41; 23:34.
79. Cf. Matt. 24:9; 10:22.
80. Cf. Matt. 13:21; 24:9, 21, 29.
81. Cf. Matt. 10:28; 24:9.
82. Cf. Matt. 25:40, 45. On the interpretation of the "parable" of the Last Judgment, cf. L. Cope, "Matthew xxv 31–46—'The Sheep and the Goats' Reinterpreted," *Novum Testamentum* 11 (1969): 37–41.
83. Cf. Matt. 13:41–43; 25:31–46.

Chapter Four

1. Cf. Matt. 1:23; also 18:20; 28:20.
2. Cf. Matt. 1:22–23; 2:15; 3:17; 11:27; 17:5.
3. Cf. Matt. 3:16–17; 11:27; 14:33; 16:16; 26:63–64; 27:54; 28:19.
4. Cf., e.g., the Sermon on the Mount: 5:16, 45, 48; 6:1, 4, 6, 8, 14, 18, 26, 32; 7:11.
5. Cf. Matt. 23:8; also 18:21, 35.
6. Cf., e.g., Matt. 8:21, 25; 14:28, 30; 16:22; 17:4; 26:22.
7. Cf. Matt. 4:18–22; also 8:21–22; 9:9.
8. Cf. Matt. 8:23; also 14:22.
9. Cf. Matt. 10:1, 5; 11:1.
10. Cf. H. Frankemölle, *Jahwebund und Kirche Christi* (NTAbh 10; Münster: Aschendorff, 1974), chap. 1.
11. Cf. Mark 5:37, 40; 14:33.
12. Cf. Mark 3:14; also 11:11; 14:17.
13. Cf. Mark 3:7; 14:14.

14. Cf. Matt. 26:69, 71; also 26:40.
15. Cf. Matt. 26:18, 20, 36; 28:20.
16. Cf. Matt. 16:21; 20:17–19.
17. Cf. Matt. 26:28 with 27:38–54.
18. Cf. Matt. 19:4, 8; 22:16.
19. Cf. Matt. 5:18; 12:5; 15:6; 22:36; 23:23.
20. Cf. Matt. 5:17; 7:12; 11:13; 22:40.
21. Cf., e.g., Davies, *The Sermon on the Mount*, 27–32.
22. Cf., e.g., Barth, "Matthew's Understanding of the Law," *Tradition and Interpretation in Matthew*, 94.
23. Cf. Exod. 20:13, 14.
24. Cf. Exod. 21:23–25; Lev. 24:19–20; Deut. 19:21.
25. Cf. Meier, *Law and History in Matthew's Gospel*, 140–56. Other important studies on the Sermon on the Mount are: Guelich, *The Sermon on the Mount*; and Betz, *Essays on the Sermon on the Mount*.
26. Cf. Exod. 20:7; 22:10–11; Lev. 19:12; Num. 5:19–22; 30:3, 16a; Deut. 6:13; 10:20; 23:21.
27. Cf. Matt. 22:16; 7:28–29.
28. Cf. Matt. 19:9; also Lev. 18:6–18.
29. Cf. Exod. 20:8–11; Deut. 5:13–14.
30. Cf. Matt. 12:7; also 9:13.
31. Cf. Matt. 12:12.
32. Cf. Matt. 3:15; 5:6, 10, 20; 6:1, 33; 21:32.
33. Cf. Matt. 6:33; also 5:6.
34. Cf. Matt. 5:20; 6:1; also 5:10.
35. Cf. Matt. 7:21; 12:50; 18:14; 21:31a.
36. Cf. Matt. 7:16–20; 12:33; 13:23; 21:43.
37. Cf. Matt. 6:2, 5, 16.
38. Cf. esp. Matt. 23:28; also 23:13, 15–16, 23, 25, 27, 29.
39. Cf. Matt. 3:7–10; 12:33–37; 23:13, 15, 27–28, 33.
40. Cf. Matt. 18:3–4, 6, 10.
41. Cf. Matt. 20:25–26.
42. Cf. Matt. 13:17; 23:29.
43. Cf. Matt. 3:2, 5–6, 11.
44. Cf. Matt. 10:40–41 with 23:34–35.
45. Cf. Matt. 13:43, 49; 25:37, 46.
46. Cf. Matt. 5:9, 45; 13:38.
47. Cf. Matt. 1:21; 26:28; 27:38–54.
48. Cf. Matt. 13:19, 23.
49. Cf. Matt. 13:8, 23; 21:43.
50. Cf. Matt. 25:21, 23.
51. Cf. Matt. 5:3, 10; 25:34.
52. Cf. Matt. 22:14; 24:22, 24, 31.
53. Cf. Matt. 13:43, 49; 25:37, 46; but cf. also 10:41.

54. Cf. Matt. 5:11–12; 10:17, 23; 13:21; 23:34.
55. Cf. Matt. 13:21; 24:9.
56. Cf. Matt. 7:15–23; 24:11.
57. Cf. Matt. 13:21; 24:9–10.
58. Cf. Matt. 24:12; also 20:15.
59. Cf. Matt. 10:23; 13:30, 39b–43, 49–50; 16:27–28; 19:28–29; 24:3, 27, 39, 42, 44; 25:31–46.
60. Cf., e.g., Matt. 5:3–10, 19–20; 6:33; 7:21; 12:40; 13:40–41; 17:9; 24:27, 37, 38–39.
61. Cf. Matt. 18:6, 8–9.
62. Cf. Matt. 24:36–39, 40–42, 43–44, 50–51; 25:11–13, 24–30.
63. Cf. Matt. 13:47–50; 24:45–51; 25:1–13, 14–30.
64. Cf. Matt. 5:12; 6:4, 6, 18; 10:41–42.
65. Cf. Matt. 10:24–25, 38–39; 16:24–26.
66. Cf. Matt. 24:45; 25:21, 23.
67. Cf. Matt. 6:10, 33; 13:44, 45–46.
68. Cf. Matt. 24:27, 32–35, 45–46; 25:10, 20–23.
69. On the community of Matthew, cf. J. D. Kingsbury, "The Verb *akolouthein* ('to follow') as an Index of Matthew's View of His Community," *Journal of Biblical Literature* 97 (1978): 56–73; Waetjen, *The Origin and Destiny of Humanness*, chap. 2; R. E. Brown and J. P. Meier, *Antioch and Rome* (New York: Paulist Press, 1983), 11–86; R. H. Smith, *Easter Gospels* (Minneapolis: Augsburg Pub., 1983), 55–67.
70. C. F. D. Moule, *The Birth of the New Testament* (Harper's New Testament Commentaries; New York: Harper & Row, 1962), 219.
71. Cf., e.g., Matt. 5:20; 6:1.
72. Cf., e.g., Matt. 13:39, 40, 49.
73. Cf. Matt. 11:22, 24; 12:36.
74. Cf. Matt. 1:1, 16, 17, 18.
75. Cf. Matt. 3:11; 11:2–3.
76. Cf. Matt. 1:1, 6, 17, 20, 25; 21:5, 9.
77. Cf. Matt. 1:23; 2:6, 15; 28:20.
78. Cf. Matt. 4:12, 18, 23.
79. Cf. Matthew 8—9; 11:23; 17:24.
80. Cf. Matt. 9:10, 28; 12:46 and 13:1; 13:36; 17:25.
81. Cf., e.g., Matt. 3:13—4:13; 8:23—9:1; 16:13–20 (but cf. 17:22).
82. Cf., e.g., Matt. 5:31–32, 33–37, 38–42; 19:3–12; 15:20.
83. Cf. Matt. 5:17–18; 24:20; 23:2–3, 23.
84. Cf. Matt. 15:2 with Mark 7:2–4.
85. Cf. Matt. 4:12, 15; 28:7, 16–20; cf. also 10:18.
86. Cf. Matt. 10:11, 14, 15, 23; 23:34; also 5:14.
87. Cf. G. D. Kilpatrick, *The Origins of the Gospel According to St. Matthew* (Oxford: Clarendon Press, 1946), 135–37.
88. Cf., e.g., Luke 7:41; 12:6, 59; 19:13.
89. Cf. Matt. 10:18, 22; 13:21; 24:9.

90. Cf. Hare, *The Theme of Jewish Persecution of Christians in the Gospel According to St. Matthew*, 106–8, 124.

91. Cf. Kingsbury, *The Parables of Jesus in Matthew 13*, 63–76.

92. Cf. Thompson, *Matthew's Advice to a Divided Community. Mt. 17,22 – 18,23*, 66–68.

93. Cf., e.g., R. Hummel, *Die Auseinandersetzung zwischen Kirche und Judentum im Matthäusevangelium* (BEvT 33; München: Kaiser, 1963), 66–75, 162–73.

94. Cf. Matt. 4:23; 9:35; 10:17; 12:9; 13:54; 23:34.

95. Cf. Kingsbury, "The Verb *akolouthein* ('to follow') as an Index of Matthew's View of His Community," 59–60.

96. Cf. Matt. 5:10–12; 10:17, 23, 28; 23:34–35.

97. Cf. Matt. 28:19–20; also 1:23; 18:20.

98. Cf. Matt. 5:9, 45; 13:38.

99. Cf. Matt. 12:49–50; 18:35; 23:8; 25:40; 28:10.

100. Cf. Matt. 18:3, 6, 10.

101. Cf. Matt. 11:29; also 10:24–25.

102. Cf. Matt. 10:41 with 10:6, 17, 23; 23:34 with 23:29a.

103. Cf. Matt. 10:41 with 10:18; 24:14; 26:13; 28:19.

104. Cf. É. Cothenet, "Les prophètes chrétiens dans l'Évangile selon saint Matthieu," *L'Évangile selon Matthieu*, ed. M. Didier (BETL 29; Gembloux: Duculot, 1972), 294.

105. Cf. U. Wilkens, "Sophia," *Theological Dictionary of the New Testament*, eds. G. Kittel and G. Friedrich (Grand Rapids: Eerdmans, 1971) VII, 505.

106. Cf. Matt. 4:18–20; 10:2; 16:16.

107. Cf. J. D. Kingsbury, "The Figure of Peter in Matthew's Gospel as a Theological Problem," *Journal of Biblical Literature* 98 (1979): 67–83.

108. Cf. G. Bornkamm, "The Authority to 'Bind' and 'Loose' in the Church in Matthew's Gospel," *Jesus and Man's Hope*, ed. D. G. Buttrick (Pittsburgh: Pittsburgh Theological Seminary, 1970) I, 37–50; R. E. Brown, K. P. Donfried, J. Reumann, eds., *Peter in the New Testament* (Minneapolis: Augsburg, 1973), 95–101.

109. Cf. Eusebius, *Ecclesiastical History*, III. 39. 16.

110. Cf. Stendahl, *The School of St. Matthew*, 30–35.

111. Cf. G. Strecker, *Der Weg der Gerechtigkeit* (FRLANT 82; Göttingen: Vandenhoeck & Ruprecht, 1962), 15–35; Meier, *The Vision of Matthew*, 17–25.

SELECTED BIBLIOGRAPHY

Bauer, David, R. "The Structure of Matthew's Gospel." Ph.D. dissertation, Union Theological Seminary in Virginia, 1985. Reviews current hypotheses on the structure of Matthew's Gospel and analyzes this structure afresh by drawing on recognizable and definable principles of rhetorical criticism.

Betz, Hans Dieter. *Essays on the Sermon on the Mount*. Philadelphia: Fortress Press, 1985. Reconstructs the Sermon on the Mount as a pre-Matthean source dating from around A.D. 50 and sees it as an epitome of the theology of Jesus written from the perspective of early Jewish Christianity.

Bornkamm, Günther, Gerhard Barth, and Heinz Joachim Held. *Tradition and Interpretation in Matthew*. Trans. P. Scott. New Testament Library. Philadelphia: Westminster Press, 1963. A collection of three studies: the first stresses that the orientation of the church in Matthean perspective is toward the future coming of Jesus as the Judge of all; the second deals with Matthew's understanding of the law; and the third discusses how Matthew interprets the miracle stories of Jesus.

Brown, Raymond E. *The Birth of the Messiah*. Garden City, N.Y.: Doubleday & Co., 1977. A commentary on the infancy narratives of Matthew and Luke which also probes the role these narratives played in the early Christian understanding of Jesus and contends that each one constitutes the essential gospel-story in miniature.

Burnett, Fred W. *The Testament of Jesus-Sophia*. Washington, D.C.: University Press of America, 1981. Argues that the "apocalyptic discourse" of Matthew (24:3–31) functions within the Gospel as a farewell speech that Jesus delivers in his capacity as Wisdom and as the (soon to be exalted) Son of man.

Cope, O. Lamar. *Matthew: A Scribe Trained for the Kingdom of Heaven.* The Catholic Biblical Quarterly Monograph Series 5. Washington, D.C.: The Catholic Biblical Association of America, 1976. Attempts to determine by a minute literary analysis of selected passages how Matthew has influenced the composition of his Gospel.

Davies, W. D. *The Setting of the Sermon on the Mount.* Cambridge, Cambridge University Press, 1964. Considers first-century influences, within both Judaism and the church, which led to the compilation and presentation of the moral teaching that is commonly known as the Sermon on the Mount.

Edwards, Richard A. *Matthew's Story of Jesus.* Philadelphia: Fortress Press, 1985. Intends to examine the narrative of Matthew from the point of view of a reader.

Ellis, Peter R. *Matthew: His Mind and His Message.* Collegeville, Minn.: Liturgical Press, 1974. Aims to reach the mind of Matthew and to ascertain the theological message he sought to communicate to his Jewish-Christian readers at the end of the first century A.D.

Garland, David E. *The Intention of Matthew 23.* Supplements to Novum Testamentum 52. Leiden: E. J. Brill, 1979. Proposes to uncover the intention Matthew pursued in writing chapter 23 by attending to the compositional makeup of the chapter and its place within the structure of the Gospel.

Gerhardsson, Birger. *The Mighty Acts of Jesus According to Matthew.* Scripta Minora. Lund: CWK Gleerup, 1979. Interprets the miracles, or "mighty acts," that Matthew depicts Jesus, or his followers, as performing in his Gospel.

Goulder, M. D. *Midrash and Lection in Matthew.* London: SPCK, 1974. Maintains that Matthew's Gospel is an adaptation and expansion of Mark's Gospel by means of midrash and was written to be read in the setting of Christian worship.

Guelich, Robert A. *The Sermon on the Mount.* Waco, Tex.: Word, 1982. A commentary on the Sermon on the Mount which views God's personal covenant through Jesus as a vantage point from which to understand the Sermon within the context of Matthew's Gospel as a whole.

Gundry, Robert H. *The Use of the Old Testament in St. Matthew's Gospel.* Supplements to Novum Testamentum 18. Leiden: E. J. Brill, 1967. Investigates the OT quotations in Matthew's Gospel with special reference to the theme of the fulfillment of messianic prophecy.

Hare, Douglas R. A. *The Theme of Jewish Persecution of Christians in the Gospel According to St. Matthew.* Society for New Testament Studies Monograph Series 6. Cambridge: Cambridge University Press, 1967. Discusses the theme of Jewish persecution of Christians at the time of Matthew and aims both to show how such persecution has influenced the theology of Matthew and to argue that it was directed primarily against Christian missionaries.

Johnson, Marshall D. *The Purpose of the Biblical Genealogies.* Society for New Testament Studies Monograph Series 8. Cambridge: Cambridge University Press, 1969. Analyzes the genealogies of Matthew and Luke and understands them to be a form of literary expression that is used to articulate the conviction that Jesus is the fulfillment of the hope of Israel.

Kingsbury, Jack Dean. *Matthew as Story.* Philadelphia: Fortress Press, 1986. Treats the gospel-story of Matthew by explaining literary-critical method, describing the major characters, and tracing the development of the story in terms of both Jesus' conflict with his Jewish opponents and his interaction with his disciples.

―――. *Matthew: Structure, Christology, Kingdom.* Philadelphia and London: Fortress Press and SPCK, 1975. Examines the structure of Matthew's Gospel and his view of the history of salvation, the titles of majesty that together constitute Matthew's portrait of Jesus, and his concept of the kingdom of heaven, in the interest of explicating the theology Matthew espouses.

―――. *The Parables of Jesus in Matthew 13.* 3d reprinted ed. London and St. Louis: SPCK and Clayton Publishing House, 1976. Investigates the eight parables that comprise Jesus' parable speech in Matthew's Gospel so as to ascertain the role this speech plays within the Gospel and to understand both Matthew's theology and the situation of his church.

Meier, John P. *Law and History in Matthew's Gospel.* Analecta Biblica 71. Rome: Biblical Institute, 1976. Plumbs the meaning of the statement on the law in Matt. 5:17–20 in the light of the antitheses that follow and within the larger context of Matthew's theology of salvation history, eschatology, and Christology.

―――. *The Vision of Matthew.* Theological Inquiries. New York: Paulist Press, 1979. A study of Matthew's Gospel in three parts: Part I introduces the reader to Matthew and his situation; Part II argues that the special characteristic of the Gospel is the nexus between Christ and church; and Part III examines the relation to Christ and the law in Matt. 5:17–20.

Mohrlang, Roger. *Matthew and Paul: A Comparison of Ethical Perspectives*. Society for New Testament Studies Monograph Series 48. Cambridge: Cambridge University Press, 1984. Compares with each other the basic structures of Matthew's and Paul's ethics, concluding that while the elements of law and grace are found in both, Matthew's emphasis is on an ethical system based on law and submission to authority.

Nolan, Brian M. *The Royal Son of God*. Orbis Biblicus et Orientalis 23. Göttingen: Vandenhoeck & Ruprecht, 1979. Argues that underlying all titles of majesty Matthew ascribes Jesus is an integrative substratum, namely, royal Davidic theology.

Senior, Donald. *The Passion of Jesus in the Gospel of Matthew*. The Passion Series 1. Wilmington: Michael Glazier, 1985. Aims to elucidate the passion narrative of Matthew's Gospel in both its historical background and its theological import as the climax of the Gospel.

Shuler, Philip L. *A Genre for the Gospels*. Philadelphia, Fortress Press, 1982. Advances the thesis that Matthew's Gospel belongs to the genre of ancient literature called encomium or laudatory biography.

Stanton, Graham, ed. *The Interpretation of Matthew*. Issues in Religion and Theology 3. Philadelphia and London: Fortress Press and SPCK, 1983. A collection of eight articles on Matthew's Gospel which have been translated from the German and are introduced by the editor.

Stendahl, Krister. *The School of St. Matthew*. Philadelphia: Fortress Press, 1968. Discusses the OT quotations in the First Gospel and a comparison of certain of the Gospel's literary features with the Habakkuk Commentary from Qumran with a view to advancing the thesis that Matthew's Gospel was used as a manual for teaching and administration within the church.

Suggs, M. Jack. *Wisdom, Christology, and Law in Matthew's Gospel*. Cambridge: Harvard University Press, 1970. Investigates the figure of Wisdom in Matthew's Gospel and aims to show that Wisdom constitutes a fundamental part of Matthew's theology and that Matthew has identified Wisdom with Christ.

Thompson, William G. *Matthew's Advice to a Divided Community: Mt. 17,22–18,35*. Analecta Biblica 44. Rome: Biblical Institute, 1970. Analyzes the structure and theology of the ecclesiological discourse and pays special attention to the many literary techniques Matthew has employed in composing this section.

Tilborg, Sjef Van. *The Jewish Leaders in Matthew.* Leiden: E. J. Brill, 1972. Studies the texts in Matthew's Gospel dealing with the Jewish leaders as an index of Matthew's relation to contemporary Judaism and concludes that Matthew regards all the Jewish leaders equally as the representatives of the one Israel his church must face.

Waetjen, Herman C. *The Origin and Destiny of Humanness.* Corte Madera, Calif.: Omega Books, 1976. Understands Matthew's Gospel as a "Book of Origin" written for the purpose of conveying to upper-class Christian Jews at home in Syrian Antioch the self-understanding that they constitute the community of Jesus, the new Human Being, who has inaugurated the new humankind.

Witherup, Ronald D. "The Cross of Jesus: A Literary-Critical Study of Matthew 27." Ph.D. dissertation, Union Theological Seminary in Virginia, 1985. Approaches Matthew 27 literary-critically and sees it as the climax of the life of Jesus which Matthew has narrated thus far in his Gospel and the place where he also brings together major themes that have appeared throughout his story.